A Man's Workbook

Previous Books by Stephanie S. Covington

Leaving the Enchanted Forest: The Path from Relationship Addiction to Intimacy

A Woman's Way Through the Twelve Steps

A Woman's Way Through the Twelve Steps Workbook

A Woman's Way Through the Twelve Steps (facilitator guide and DVD)

La Mujer Y Su Practica de los Doce Pasos

Awakening Your Sexuality: A Guide for Recovering Women

Women in Recovery: Understanding Addiction

Mujeres en recuperación: Entendiendo la adicción

Beyond Trauma: A Healing Journey for Women (facilitator guide, workbook, and DVDs)

Voices: A Program of Self-Discovery and Empowerment for Girls (facilitator guide and workbook)

Women and Addiction: A Gender-Responsive Approach (manual and DVD)

Helping Women Recover: A Program for Treating Addiction (facilitator's guide and woman's journal)

Helping Women Recover: A Program for Treating Substance Abuse: Special Edition for Use in the Criminal Justice System (facilitator's guide and woman's journal)

Previous Books by Dan Griffin

A Man's Way Through the Twelve Steps

A Man's Workbook

A PROGRAM FOR TREATING ADDICTION

Special Edition for Use in the Criminal Justice System

Stephanie S. Covington, Dan Griffin,
and Rick Dauer

JOSSEY-BASS
A Wiley Imprint
www.josseybass.com

Published by Jossey-Bass
A Wiley Imprint
989 Market Street, San Francisco, CA 94103-1741—www.josseybass.com

Jossey-Bass books and products are available through most bookstores. To contact Jossey-Bass directly call our Customer Care Department within the U.S. at 800-956-7739, outside the U.S. at 317-572-3986, or fax 317-572-4002.

Jossey-Bass also publishes its books in a variety of electronic formats. Some content that appears in print may not be available in electronic books.

ISBN 978-0-470-48656-6

Printed in the United States of America
FIRST EDITION
PB Printing   SKY10026442_042221

CONTENTS

Appendix: Materials Related to Recovery 223

A Man's
Workbook

About This Program

Helping Men Recover addresses issues that many men struggle with, especially if they are experiencing problems with alcohol or other drugs. You are reading this because you are considering, or have decided to make, fundamental changes in your life. In most cases, you will be using this workbook as part of a program in which you meet regularly with a group of other recovering men. You will attend eighteen sessions with them; together, you will develop new skills and new ways of thinking about yourselves as men. Your group will be led by a facilitator who has experience with addiction therapy and the process of recovery. He will offer you insights about the thoughts and feelings that you may experience as you do the work suggested in the sessions and in this workbook. Although this workbook is designed for use in the *Helping Men Recover* program, you may use it one-on-one with an addictions counselor, other therapist, or a member of a correctional staff.

The program is organized into four sections, or modules: Self, Relationships, Sexuality, and Spirituality. These are four areas that men consistently identify as the triggers for relapse and the areas of greatest change in their recoveries. Within the four modules, specific topics are covered, including

- Self-awareness and identity
- How men are socialized in our society
- The impact of the family of origin
- Grounding and relaxation techniques
- Communication
- Power, violence, and abuse
- Relationships
- Trauma and addiction
- Sexual identity
- Healthy sexuality
- What spirituality is

1

The Spiral of Addiction and Recovery

Addiction is a downward spiral. Recovery, in contrast, is like an upward spiral, away from a life that revolves around the objects of addiction (alcohol or other drugs, sex, gambling, and so forth) and outward into ever-widening circles of freedom, self-knowledge, and connection with others.

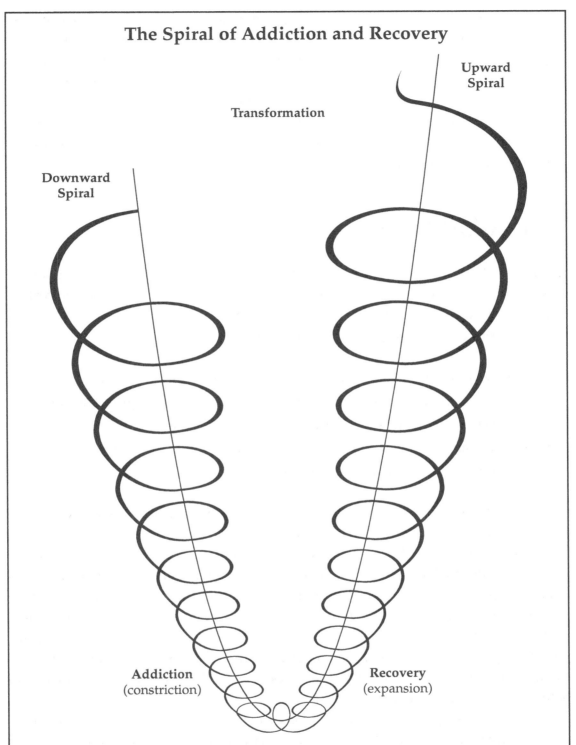

The Spiral of Addiction and Recovery

Upward Spiral

Transformation

Downward Spiral

Addiction (constriction)

Recovery (expansion)

From *Helping Women Recover: A Program for Treating Addiction* (rev. ed.), by Stephanie S. Covington, 2008. San Francisco: Jossey-Bass. Copyright 2008 by Stephanie S. Covington. Reprinted with permission.

Each man's process of recovery is unique, but most of us find that it involves discovering our true selves, connecting in healthy relationships with others, understanding our sexuality, and gaining some spiritual connection. Awareness is the first step toward change. When you become aware of your addiction, you can decide to begin a process of recovery. When you become more aware of yourself and your relationships, you can make changes in your life. So the journey is about discovery as well as recovery. As you begin to think, feel, and act differently, you begin to heal and to connect with and value all parts of yourself—inner as well as outer.

This Workbook

A Man's Workbook is for recording your experiences during this program. Using this workbook will help you to reflect on and remember what you learn, think, and feel during the group sessions and as you continue to practice the skills of recovery on your own between sessions. This workbook contains

- Summaries of information that you will receive in the group sessions
- Some of the activities and exercises that you will do during the group sessions
- Activities for you to work on between the group sessions
- Questionnaires that will help you to track your progress in recovery
- Space for you to reflect on what you learned in each session

The activities that are to be completed between the group sessions are designed to help you to reflect on what you have learned and to put some new skills and behaviors into practice. Men learn best by doing, and these activities also help you to see the benefits of what you are practicing. The activities are not things you have to do in order to pass a class. Some of them involve writing or drawing exercises, but your skills in these areas are not being tested. You do not need to worry about your handwriting or spelling. What matters is what you put into the activities and, consequently, what you get out of them. There are no right or wrong answers, no "shoulds" or "shouldn'ts," and your work will not be checked or graded. This workbook is a tool to help you with your growth and recovery.

There will be opportunities during some group sessions for you to share what you have written in your workbook. You can share what you want and keep the rest private. The group meeting is a safe place, and there will be ground rules regarding confidentiality.

4

You can use this workbook to highlight what you want to remember from each module and to make notes about what you are thinking and feeling as you go through this program.

You may be concerned about keeping your workbook private. If you live with others and are not sure that they will respect your privacy, you should hide your workbook or lock it up. Or you can ask the facilitator or another counselor to help you find a way to keep your workbook safe between group sessions. The facilitator is prepared for such requests. If the facilitator will be holding your workbook between the sessions, he will respect your privacy and will arrange for you to complete the extra activities after each session or at some other time.

If you are living in a jail or prison, your facilitator will offer guidelines on how to use this workbook and how to keep it safe.

MODULE A

Self

SESSION I

Defining Self

The Journey Ahead

In the process of recovery, you will spiral through the question "Who am I?" many times. Each time, you grow closer to knowing who you really are and have another opportunity to let go of who you are not. In early recovery, you will need to begin with the acknowledgment "I am an alcoholic" or "I am an addict." This becomes an essential part of your identity, although not all of it by any means. Breaking through denial about addiction to alcohol and other drugs (or other compulsive behaviors) is difficult for anyone. What may seem hardest is accepting that there is something you cannot figure out or control. The acknowledgment that you are an addict is the beginning of your opportunity to look at every aspect of what it means to be a man in our culture and to determine what you want to accept and what you want to reject. Ultimately, you get to choose who you want to be as a man and even who you want to be as a man in recovery.

Part of exploring one's self is recognizing what one feels. Men who have problems with alcohol and other drugs often don't know what they are feeling and have limited vocabularies for describing their feelings. Feelings are not "manly." Anger, indifference, and sarcasm often become the catch-alls for the variety of feelings men have. Yet these can damage a man's relationships as well as his physical, mental, and spiritual health. Therefore, in this module, you will be asked, "What are you feeling?" and "How did you feel?" Learning the language of feelings is an essential part of recovery. It is also the foundation for developing healthy, intimate relationships.

Group Agreements

At the beginning of Session 1, your facilitator will explain some group agreements that will be maintained during the group sessions. When everyone agrees to them, the sessions will have the most benefit for all group members. Typical group agreements are listed here for your reference; the ones presented in your session may differ somewhat because of the requirements of the program sponsors.

1. **Attendance**. We're all committing to show up at all the sessions. Your commitment to attend regularly helps to stabilize the group and creates an environment of mutual support. If you must miss a group meeting, please let the facilitator know well in advance of that session. If you end up missing too many sessions, it may affect your ability to stay in the group.

2. **Confidentiality**. No personal information revealed in this room is to be repeated outside the room. We need to know that we can trust one another, and there can be no trust if information about a group member is given to outsiders or if group members gossip about one another outside the group. There are two exceptions to this rule of confidentiality: (1) The facilitator may have to communicate with other members of your treatment teams as part of your ongoing care; and (2) the facilitator is required by law to break confidentiality when a member's personal safety or the safety of another person is at stake. You, as group members, will be responsible for maintaining confidentiality among yourselves.

3. **Safety**. It is important that each of you feels safe in this group. It is not easy for men to admit when they do not feel safe. We do not often talk about safety. You may be thinking that safety is about defending yourself or protecting yourself from harm. But safety is also about feeling emotionally safe, feeling grounded and comfortable when sharing your thoughts and problems with others. The facilitator's commitment is to make sure that this is a safe group, and he needs that same commitment from each of you. In order for this to happen, all group members need to agree that there will be no verbal or physical abuse here.

4. **Participation**. Everyone should have a chance to join in the discussion. It is not helpful if some people dominate the conversation and if others remain silent. Also, please share all remarks with the whole group. Your comments, questions, and opinions are of interest to all members, and side remarks from one individual to another tend to distract and divide the group. Sometimes the facilitator will ask a question and want everyone to respond. He may call on you to respond to a specific question or share about a certain topic. We would all like

to hear what you have to say. However, if you are unwilling to talk about a particular subject, you always have the option to "pass."

5. **Honesty**. We're here to tell the truth. Nobody will pressure you to tell anything about yourself that you don't want to talk about, but when you do talk, tell the truth about where you've been and how you feel. The facilitator may ask questions to better understand what you are saying or support you in telling your whole truth. It will be more helpful if you talk about your personal experiences, rather than about people in general, so speak with "I" statements rather than saying "you" or "we."

6. **Respect**. When you tell the truth about what you think, please do so in a way that respects others in the group. That means no criticizing, judging, or talking down to anyone. If you think that someone is showing disrespect to someone else, please say so respectfully. If someone is dominating the conversation, the facilitator will referee so that everyone gets a chance to talk. If you think he is not doing his job as a referee, let him know. If you feel uncomfortable or angry at some point and do not want to participate, do not disrupt the group. You can choose to be quiet until you feel more comfortable and are ready to participate again.

7. **Questions**. There are no dumb questions or wrong answers, as long as you speak about what is true for you. Ask whatever is on your mind. Please respect one another's honest questions and opinions.

8. **Staying on Task**. We're here to talk about a program of recovery. Please stick to that topic. If we start to go off task, the facilitator will direct us back to the topic at hand. If you think that we're getting off the topic and he's not doing anything about it, or if you think that he's headed off on a tangent, please feel free to refocus us.

9. **Punctuality**. We'll start on time and end on time. The times of our group sessions are _____. If you are late to the group, we will start without you. The facilitator may also challenge you to be accountable for being late. Being late is almost always a choice and an expression of how you are conducting yourself in recovery.

10. **Abstinence**. We do not want to assume that there are any expectations for this group that are simply "understood." It is important to be abstinent (or sober) when you come to each session. If you come while under the influence, the facilitator will ask you to leave that day, and your status in the program will be evaluated. If you use mood-altering chemicals between treatment sessions, it is essential that you inform the facilitator or another staff person as soon as possible.

Feeling Okay

There are times when you may feel uncomfortable or anxious in the group. This happens to everyone at various times, especially in unfamiliar settings and with new experiences. A lot of the time, we keep these feelings to ourselves. We do not know how to deal with excitement, anxiety, and feeling uncomfortable, so we attempt to relieve our discomfort by using alcohol or other drugs. Here are three techniques that you can use at any time to help you to relax or calm yourself and feel more grounded. Being grounded means detaching from your inner, emotional discomfort by becoming more aware of the physical world and being present in the here and now. These exercises will help you to deal with your feelings, so that they do not control your behavior and take you back to using.

Palms Up/Palms Down

1. Sit up straight in your seat, with both feet on the floor and your eyes closed.
2. Hold both your arms outstretched, with the palms of your hands turned up and touching side by side, as though someone was about to put something in your hands.
3. Visualize a list of all the thoughts and feelings that are bothering you right now.
4. Now imagine placing all your cares, concerns, problems, troubles, and painful memories into your hands. All these negative emotions and thoughts are out of your body and lying in your hands.
5. Imagine the weight of holding all these problems, these negative thoughts and emotions, in your hands. Feel the strain of carrying them.
6. Go back inside yourself and find any remaining pain, discomfort, and stress. Then slowly move these sensations out through your arms and into your hands.
7. You may feel the weight of the emotional and physical distress pushing down on your hands.
8. Now, slowly and carefully turn your hands upside down, so that your palms face the floor. Let all the problems, stresses, bad feelings, and negativity fall to the floor. For now, drop your burdens.

Relaxation

1. Relax again. Take a deep breath. Let it out.
2. You are going to tense up certain parts of your body and then let the tension go. If you want to make a sound when you are letting the tension go, that may help you to connect more to your body.

3. Hold your hands out in front of you. Make a fist as tight as you can. Now, open your hands and let them relax.

4. Now tense your arms . . . and relax.

5. Now tense your feet . . . and relax.

6. Tense your legs . . . and relax.

7. Tense your stomach . . . and relax.

8. Tense your jaw . . . and relax.

9. Tense the muscles in your face . . . and relax.

10. Now see if you can tense your whole body.

11. And relax it.

Deep Breathing

Another helpful exercise is learning to take very deep breaths, from all the way down in your abdomen, not just from your upper chest.

1. Put one hand on your chest and one hand on your stomach.

2. Take a couple of normal breaths. You probably will find that you are feeling these breaths mostly in your chest.

3. Try moving your breath deeper into your lower abdomen, so that your hand on your stomach moves as you breathe.

4. Close your mouth and press your tongue lightly to the roof of your mouth. Let your jaw relax.

5. Take a breath slowly in through your nose, counting to three.

6. Slowly exhale and feel the breath leaving your nose as you count to three one more time.

7. This exercise is called Deep Breathing. Try it again. You will find that you are breathing more slowly and more completely than usual.

8. As thoughts come up, acknowledge them and then return your focus to your breathing.

9. Keep breathing deeply, but blow the air out of your mouth, rather than out of your nose. Let your abdomen fill with air each time.

The goal of relaxation and grounding exercises is to get your mind off other concerns and help keep you focused on what you are trying to accomplish. Learning how to calm ourselves when emotions start to take over is a skill that we all can use. You can use these techniques when you are feeling stressed or uncomfortable. Practicing these grounding exercises between the sessions will help them to become easier and more natural for you.

What Do You Want to Get out of This Group?

You are probably using this workbook because alcohol or other drugs have been causing you serious problems. Recovery is about taking responsibility for how you feel, how you act, and how you relate with others. This program will help you realize that, although you can't always control what happens to you, you do get to decide what kind of man you become.

Please think about what you want to get out of the group experience. Think about what you really want, not what your counselor, a judge, your partner, your employer, or anyone else wants. What do you need to accomplish in order to become the man you always knew you could be? Sobriety is a great answer but it should not be your only answer.

1. What do you want to get out of the group experience?

2. What do you think you will need from the rest of the group in order to get what you want?

3. What can you do to help yourself get what you want?

Introduction to Feelings

Whether we like it or not, our feelings are essential parts of who we are. How we respond to our feelings is an important issue for men. Denying our bad feelings or trying to get away from them by using alcohol and other drugs does not make them go away. Using doesn't help to keep the good feelings, either.

As a result of the work you do in this session, you may experience some intense feelings over the next weeks and months that have been avoided and denied for a long time. Becoming more aware of your feelings and responding to them appropriately will be critical to your staying sober and achieving a meaningful recovery.

Name the two or three feelings that are the most difficult for you to handle effectively. You may refer to page 19 to help you get started in answering this.

As you continue in the program, try to be aware of when you are experiencing these feelings and ask for support in learning how to cope with them in a healthy manner.

Who Am I?

Most of us have been taught to think of ourselves in terms of our roles as providers, fathers, husbands, relationship partners, employees, teammates, and so on. There is nothing wrong with this—in fact, our connections with others tell us much about who we are. However, our roles do not tell the whole story about who we are. In recovery, it is important to develop our relationships with others—our outer selves—and our relationship with our inner selves—our thoughts, feelings, values, and beliefs.

We are often uncomfortable focusing on our relationships and our inner selves. We may have been brought up to consider these things to be unmasculine. So we ignore how we feel and how the other people in our lives feel. We focus on work, sports, or possessions and tend to define ourselves according to our successes in these areas.

The questions in this section will help you begin to get to know yourself and your fellow group members better.

1. Think back to when you were about ten years old. How would someone who knew you at that age have described you?

2. Think of three things about you *now* that answer the question "Who am I?" Here's the hard part: none of your answers can refer to your work or your identity as a husband, boyfriend, son, lover, or partner. This isn't about the sports you play or your favorite leisure activities. Think about qualities or characteristics that you have. You may want to refer to the Possibilities Page (page 19) to help you answer this question and the next one.

3. In the group, you were asked to share three words that describe who you are. These can be your feelings or beliefs or qualities. For instance, a feeling might be "I feel angry." A belief might be "I believe it is important to work hard." A quality might be "I am funny" or "I like to play basketball." In the space provided on this page and the next, please add to your list of three words. Try to write twenty sentences that describe your thoughts, feelings, beliefs, and qualities. You can again use the Possibilities Page (page 19) to find words to help you describe your inner self.

1.

2.

3.

4.

5.

6.

7.

8.

9.

10.

11.

12.

13.

14.

15.

16.

17.

18.

19.

20.

Possibilities Page

Feelings	Beliefs	Qualities
angry	honesty is best	sense of humor
joyful	family is important	dependable
sad	loyalty is important	sincere
anxious	hard work is good for you	good-natured
thoughtful	monogamy is best	trustworthy
nervous	there is a God	smart
happy	save the earth	compassionate
afraid	save money	streetwise
amused	stay young at heart	gentle
hurt	fatherhood is rewarding	strong
bitter	life is tough	creative
jealous	expect the best	survivor
calm	you are what you eat	wise
lonely	anger is dangerous	funny
mad	have safe sex	warm
contented	reincarnation happens	honest
miserable	don't trust the government	passionate
disappointed	think before you speak	resilient
pleased	trust your friends	sensible
discouraged	I'm full of good ideas	energetic
depressed	I'm good with words	brave
relieved	I'm good with numbers	quick learner
embarrassed	I'm good at making things	sensitive
grateful	I'm good at fixing things	tough
grieving	I'm capable of changing	determined
ashamed	I'm a good listener	attractive

Answering these questions is a good start in exploring your inner self. As you continue in this program, you will learn much more about who you are and who you want to be. In the space provided on this page and the next, and over the course of your work in this program, you can record all the insights that you gain about yourself. Write down things that you learn in group sessions, things that you learn from the other men in your group, things that you learn from this workbook, and any other thoughts or feelings you have between sessions.

1.

2.

3.

4.

5.

6.

7.

8.

9.

10.

11.

12.

13.

14.

15.

16.

17.

18.

19.

20.

How Do I Want Others to See Me?

When there is a difference between how we want others to see us and how we see ourselves, we dedicate our energy toward creating fronts and avoiding being genuine with most, if not all, of the people in our lives. We forget how to be real. Especially if we feel shame about some part of who we are, we usually try to hide it. Then our inside and outside selves become disconnected.

Complete these three unfinished statements:

1. I want others to see me as . . .

2. I'm concerned that others may see me as . . .

3. Right now, I see myself as . . .

Assignment

At the end of each session, you will be given an assignment to be completed by the next session. These assignments are designed to help you practice the new skills that you have learned. It is important that you put your best effort into these and come prepared next time to share what you have accomplished. In addition, practicing the grounding exercise will also be helpful.

The assignment to be completed before the next session follows:

> Choose a friend, a trusted advisor, or a family member who is not aware that you are in treatment. Tell this person a little bit about why you have entered this program. Ask this person if it would be all right for you to keep him (or her) informed about what you are learning and how you are doing. At the beginning of the next session, you will describe who you talked to and how it went.

Reflections on Recovery

In this session, you have begun the process of looking at yourself and answering the question "Who am I?" This task will take you on a journey of exploring your inner feelings, thoughts, and beliefs, as well as looking at your relationships and the roles you play. The group will create a safe place in which you can learn to trust and, with the help of other men, begin to get clearer pictures of yourself. You may even get a glimpse of what your true purpose in life is.

This session is the beginning of an ongoing process. There is no miracle cure for addiction and no quick fix for most of the problems caused by addiction. But this program will give you many tools and techniques that you can use in your recovery even after you have completed the program.

Use the space that follows to record any thoughts you have about the material covered in this session.

Into Action

During this program, the facilitator and the group will talk about a lot of topics that may be new for you and may feel uncomfortable or be confusing. Every one of these topics is connected to your recovery. Being in this program is a little bit like being in a laboratory; you get to experiment with new ideas and behaviors. Some of these you will want to practice in your daily life to see if they work for you. Practicing also will help you to take advantage of one of your great qualities as a man: your ability to take action. Taking action allows you to learn. As you learn, what seems foreign or difficult will become natural to you. Even if you currently are living in a jail or prison, you can find some ways to practice new behaviors. Ask your facilitator to help you come up with some ideas. The Into Action activity is an optional assignment but it is a great way for you to practice the behaviors that ultimately will help you to stay sober.

If you choose to take some specific action between now and the next session, use the space below to describe what that action step will be. You also can record what results were achieved. Your action step can relate to a topic that was covered in Session 1 or it can be some other activity or behavioral change related to your recovery.

Examples of action steps are

- Practicing one of the relaxation/grounding exercises every day
- Making a commitment to eat healthier foods
- Making a commitment to exercise at least three times per week
- Taking a few minutes each evening to talk about your day with your partner if possible, or a friend.

Recovery Scale

Please take a few moments to mark the degree to which you do each of the following things. You can make an "X" or a circle on each line to indicate your response.

    You will complete this form again at the end of this module on Self to see how you have changed. You will not have to compare your answers with anyone else in the group, nor will you be judged on how well you are doing. This is not a test but an opportunity for you to chart your own progress in recovery.

	Not at All	Just a Little	Pretty Much	Very Much
1. I keep up my physical appearance.				
2. I exercise regularly.				
3. I eat healthy meals.				
4. I get restful sleep.				
5. I regularly go to work/school.				
6. I can adapt to change.				
7. I keep up my living space.				
8. I take constructive criticism well.				
9. I can accept praise.				
10. I laugh at funny things.				
11. I acknowledge my needs and feelings.				
12. I engage in new interests.				
13. I can relax without alcohol or drugs.				
14. I value myself.				

Men in Recovery

What Does It Mean to Be a Man?

You may not have spent a lot of time thinking about your beliefs regarding what it means to be a man. For some of us, life up to this point has not involved any serious reflection about who we are *as men*. If being sober is your priority, you will benefit from looking at how your ideas and society's ideas about masculinity could interfere with your recovery. We learn rules about what it means to be a man from our parents, other family members, teachers, coaches, friends, and so forth. We also learn some of the rules about masculinity from books, movies, and television shows. Some of these rules may be very healthy and productive for you, but some of them may impair your ability to fully realize your potential.

The "Rules" About Being a Man

1. In the space below, list all the "rules" about being a man that you can come up with. Include some of the things you were told or taught as a boy growing up. Examples are "Men should never show weakness," and "Men should take care of their partners."

Now think about what it means to be in recovery. This may still be a new concept for you, but recovery is going to be the foundation of your new life. From what was discussed in the group and what you have learned in other treatment groups or at any Twelve Step meetings you have attended, what do you think are the main principles of being in recovery? What do you need to do to stay sober? Examples are "It's important to build a support system and use it," and "It's necessary to accept responsibility for my actions."

2. In the space below, list as many principles of recovery as you can.

You probably have recognized that some of the traditional ideas about being a man are consistent with being in recovery and some of them can hinder or complicate your recovery. You may realize that, in order to be in recovery, you are being asked to do some things that conflict with your ideas about what is manly. You will have to choose whether being sober is more important than following the rules that you have adopted or taken on about being a man.

You may be ready right now to let go of your old ideas about masculinity or you may be willing to let go of some, but not all, of them. You may be unwilling to abandon any of the rules at this time.

3. Write down the rules that you are willing to abandon or change.

A Man's Workbook

4. Write down the rules that you want to hold on to for now.

Remember, recovery is a process and we all struggle with making changes. No one is asking you to become a completely different person overnight. But we do strongly encourage you to "try on" new behaviors and ideas. You may find that these fit you much better than the ones you've been wearing for a long time.

Growing Up Male

Before you began this program, how much time had you spent thinking about the beliefs and rules you have about being a man?

From the moment you were born, people started treating you differently than they treated girls. Societies have ideas about what "manhood" is and they treat boys accordingly. We develop our self-images, in part, by learning from other men and women how we are "supposed" to be. At some point, we decided that there are rules about being a man. We may not even be sure where we got all these rules but we have been following them for a long time, and they have had a lot of influence on our lives. It is important, at this point, to examine our rules and decide whether they are true—whether they help us to be what we want and to get what we want.

For a typical male in our society, a lot of the rules are "should nots": you should not show weakness; you should not ask for help; you should not talk about how you feel; you especially should not be afraid. When you do something that you are not "supposed" to do, others may criticize or shame you.

If we break—or see other men breaking—the rules, we react with judgments and assumptions. We may make fun of the other males or we may even hurt them physically. But—and this is interesting—*we do not necessarily question the rules!* The point is that a lot of us know how we are *not* supposed to act. But what about how we *can* live our lives?

Assignment

The assignment to be completed before the next session follows:

Review the list you made on page 29 of the principles of recovery. Choose one of these principles and make an effort to put it into practice between now and the next session. Be conscious on a daily basis of applying this principle to your life. Be prepared to talk about your efforts at the beginning of the next session.

Reflections on Recovery

We are not implying that all your beliefs and rules about being a man do not work for you. Many of them do. Some beliefs that work for you may not work for other men. The purpose of this session is to help you to start thinking more consciously about your beliefs about being a man. In doing so, you can actually choose what kind of man you want to be, rather than feeling compelled to live up to others' expectations. You may not change from the man you are today, but at least you will be aware of the options available to you.

Use the space below to record any thoughts you have about the material covered in today's session.

Into Action

Remember that this is an optional activity. What you choose to do does not necessarily have to relate directly to the material covered in this session; however, it should relate in some way to your recovery.

Use the space below to describe what action step you will take between now and the next session. You also can record what results were achieved.

SESSION 3

Sense of Self

A Man's Journey

We can think of our lives as journeys from birth to where we are now and to where we will be in the future. The landmarks of our journeys are

- People we have encountered along the way, such as mothers, fathers, grandparents, teachers, sexual partners, friends, and counselors
- Events we have been involved in, including one-time occurrences, such as births, accidents, and maybe even being arrested
- Experiences we have had (for example, isolation in high school, vacations with family members, and being drunk or high)

Part of exploring who we are today is to go back and look at the people, events, and experiences that have shaped us. Sometimes looking at the past can be painful. We have experienced a lot of things that we would rather forget. But remembering is important because, if we are cut off from our pasts, we're cut off from parts of ourselves. Also, examining our pasts can help us to identify things that we want to be different in the future. The good news is that we can make choices today that will improve our lives six months or a year from now. The past has shaped us but it doesn't have to control us. We can shape our presents and our futures through the choices that we make now.

1. On the next three pages, list the people, events, and experiences that have played major roles in creating who you are today. You can write in words and phrases or draw pictures or symbols.

People

<table>
<tr><td align="center">**Examples**</td></tr>
<tr><td>

My dad—an angry and violent man

The guys I met in the Army

My first girlfriend, who broke my heart

</td></tr>
</table>

Events

Examples

Losing my virginity

Buying our first house

Being arrested and going to jail

Experiences

Examples

Moving around a lot as a child

Becoming addicted to pain medications

Going back to school and starting a new career

---

2. Look back over the three lists you've created. Think about strengths you have developed through the people, events, and experiences in your life. Use the space below to list some of those strengths.

Assignment

The assignment to be completed before the next session follows:

Spend at least another thirty minutes adding to your lists of people, events, and experiences that have shaped your life.

Reflections on Recovery

You may have been raised to believe that differences between people are negative. You may feel threatened by those who look or act different from you or have different belief systems. You may also feel a sense of shame if your appearance, actions, and beliefs are not considered "normal" by the majority. In this group, we want to respect and even celebrate the differences between us. It is these differences that make us all unique individuals, and together we form a rich and powerful community of men.

Often, our life stories are based on our jobs, our families, our possessions, or our criminal histories. A more meaningful way to define ourselves is through the qualities we possess and the values we have. Please think about how you would like to define yourself, write the answer down, and bring it to the next session. One way to consider this would be to think of what you would like people to say about you at your funeral.

Use the space below to record any thoughts you have about the material covered in today's session.

Into Action

This is an optional activity. What you choose to do does not necessarily have to relate directly to the material covered in this session; however, it should relate in some way to your recovery.

Use the space below to describe what action step you will take between now and the next session. You also can record what results were achieved.

SESSION 4

Men: Inside and Out

A House Divided

Abraham Lincoln said, "A house divided against itself cannot stand." Many people are like houses divided. We are all composed of the selves we show to the world (our "outer selves," or the "outsides" of our houses) and the selves we keep from almost everyone else, if not everyone else (our "inner selves," or the "insides" of our houses).

We keep our "outer selves," or the outsides of our houses, looking a certain way, because these are the sides we show to others. These outer parts are the images we create through our behaviors, our possessions, our clothes, and our relationships. We want others to admire our houses, so we tend to "decorate" our outer selves, to present desired images to the rest of the world.

Our inner selves consist of our thoughts, feelings, values, and beliefs. You began thinking about your inner selves in Session 1, when you looked at the Possibilities Page and thought of words to answer the question "Who am I?" from a personal standpoint.

The chances are that you have paid a lot more attention to the outside of your house than to the inside. You've probably done more to maintain the outside than the inside. You probably wouldn't want us to visit the inside. The biggest problem is that *you* have to live inside your house, and when you don't take care of it, it's hard for you to stay healthy. Addiction makes a mess of the inside, and you may come to believe that you don't deserve any better. Think about these questions:

43

1. How has addiction affected you on the inside?
2. For how much of your life have you neglected the person inside?
3. How much do you hide the man you are inside from others?

You deserve to feel good about both the outside and the inside of your house. You cannot put all your energy into trying to prop up your outside while you slowly allow the inside to crumble.

You will be well served by dedicating at least as much attention to the man on the inside as you do to the man on the outside. This program will give you some tools to help you care for your inner self. The man on the outside will then become much easier to take care of. Who you are on the outside and the inside will fit together much better. You will not feel like a house divided anymore, and you will no longer fear the prospect of others getting too close and seeing the real you.

On the following pages are drawings of two houses. The first drawing represents the outside of your house—that part of yourself that you show to the world. Write descriptions on this drawing of the way you think others see you. Describe what you and other people see when they look at your exterior. This description should have positive as well as negative things.

The second drawing represents the inside of your house—the thoughts, feelings, beliefs, and personal qualities that you keep to yourself, hidden from view. Write on this drawing about who you are on the inside. What don't other people see? This description also should have positive as well as negative things.

The Outside of Your House

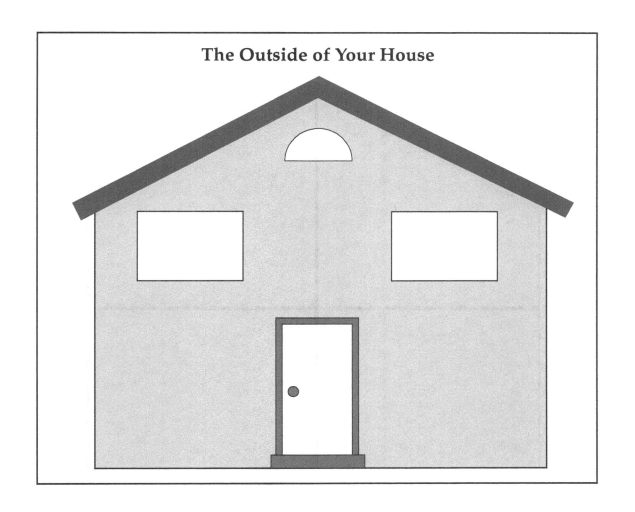

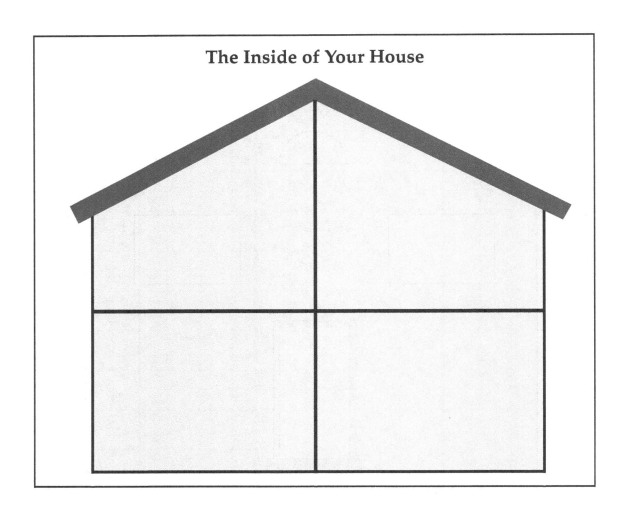

The Inside of Your House

1. What are some of the features of the outside of your house that you are proud of and would like to maintain?

2. What are some of the features of the outside of your house that are unnecessary and that you would be willing to discard?

3. What are some of the things on the inside of your house that you are proud of and would like to maintain?

4. What are some of the things on the inside of your house that work against you and that you would like to discard or change?

Assignment

The assignment to be completed before the next session follows:

Do something that will improve the inside of your house, such as writing a list of all your resentments, going to an extra A.A. or N.A. meeting, apologizing to someone, or making a commitment to be more honest with others. You will be asked to talk about this at the beginning of the next session.

Reflections on Recovery

In this session, you have begun the process of looking at how you appear to others versus how you perceive yourself and your experiences. It can be tough to look at the inner parts of ourselves, especially the parts that we keep from others. A lot of men simply ignore their inner houses, hoping that all the effort and money they invest in the outsides will compensate for what's missing on the insides. But the more attention you give to the inside of your house (the inner you), the more comfortable you will feel inviting others in to be with you. Recovery is an endeavor that works best from the inside out. Recovery is also about having the inner self and the outer self connected and congruent.

Use the space that follows to record any thoughts you have about the material covered in today's session.

Into Action

Remember that this is an optional activity and that what you choose to do does not necessarily have to relate directly to the material covered in this session; however, it should relate in some way to your recovery.

Use the space below to describe what action step you will take between now and the next session. You also can record what results were achieved.

A Man's Workbook

Men and Feelings

Men, Relationships, and Feelings

Communicating your feelings may not be easy or comfortable for you. We all experience a range of feelings, including fear, sadness, hurt, joy, shame, and anger. Our feelings mean nothing about our manliness. Our feelings are there simply to help us experience life more fully. They are essential parts of who we are. So when we ignore our feelings or are disconnected from them, we miss out on an important part of life.

The activities that you have worked on over the past several sessions have brought up feelings for you, whether you were immediately aware of them or not. The feelings or your awareness of them may not have come to the surface until later in the day or even another day. I hope that you have allowed yourself to experience those feelings and that you have made the effort to acknowledge them to yourself and perhaps to another person. The more you share such feelings with people you trust (especially your partner, as long as you do it in a safe way), the more comfortable you will be on the "inside of your house." When you have supportive people in your life who honor your feelings, you realize that they not only don't make you less of a man, they make you feel more like a man than you may have ever felt before. You will also increase the sense of connection that is the foundation for healthy and rewarding relationships.

1. What role do you think your feelings have played in your addiction? Record your answer below.

2. How have your feelings and your ability to share them with your partner affected your relationships? What have been the positive effects? What have been the negative effects? What feelings have you kept hidden from your partner? Record your answers below.

The Anger Funnel

Of all the feelings we have been talking about, anger is the one most commonly associated with men. Every man has a relationship with anger, and it usually comes down to two issues. The first is avoiding anger for fear that you'll lose your temper or go off into an uncontrollable rage—perhaps even become violent. The second is living in a continual state of resentment because you never express your anger (and maybe any other feeling).

The truth about feeling angry is that frequently the real emotion is not anger. Most anger is what counselors often call a surface or secondary emotion. There often is a more genuine and core feeling underneath. For example, imagine that your partner calls you a rude name and then makes fun of your social background. Or that you have been turned down for one job after another. Or that a friend does not return your phone calls. Most of us are conditioned to respond with anger. But if we look a little closer, we can recognize that what we are really feeling is another emotion: hurt.

For most men, there was a point early in our lives when we realized that it was not okay—or even safe—to express fear, hurt, or sadness. So we often substituted anger. The anger funnel is a symbolic representation of how our true feelings become transformed into anger. We pour all our emotions into this funnel, and anger is the only thing that comes out the other end. Then we think we will be safe. Anger becomes a protective shield. We never deal with the underlying, genuine emotion; we don't talk about the fear, the hurt, or the sadness.

You will feel justifiable anger at various times for the rest of your life. It is when we act on our anger in a way that harms other people that we need to pay attention. When anger is misused, it is about exerting power over others and attempting to control situations. When we try to do that, we frequently find ourselves getting into trouble.

A lot of men have a hard time distinguishing between anger and rage. Rage is a destructive feeling that comes from feeling a loss of control (and, often, isolated and ashamed). Rage can cause serious harm, even if it does not result in physical violence.

As we discussed in Session 1, shame and addiction go hand in hand. A lot of anger and rage is driven by shame. Much of the shame connected to addiction is the message that, not only did you make a mistake, *you are the mistake*! You did not just do something wrong; everything about you is wrong. When you experience chronic shame, it is very likely that you will not only feel disconnected from others, you will also act in self-destructive ways.

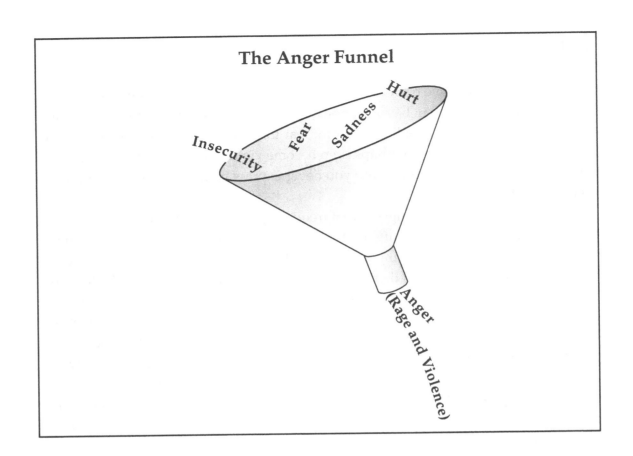

The Anger Funnel

Insecurity   Fear   Sadness   Hurt

Anger
(Rage and Violence)

1. All of us have experienced situations in which our feelings were hurt, and, rather than admit this, we responded with anger. In the spaces below, describe a specific situation in which this happened. How did it affect you? Did it have any effect on another person? How did you feel about yourself afterward?

Situation:

Feelings:

How I acted:

How it affected me:

How it affected the other person:

How I felt afterward:

2. The next time you experience a feeling that men are not commonly allowed to show—such as hurt, sadness, fear, or insecurity—pay attention to it. Make an effort to acknowledge this feeling to yourself and to another person. In the spaces below, record what happened and how you felt afterward.

Situation:

Feeling:

What happened when I shared the feeling:

How I felt afterward:

Assignment

The assignment to be completed before the next session follows:

Complete the following sentences as honestly as you can. You will not be asked to share these with anyone else.

1. One thing about my past behavior that I am very ashamed of is . . .

2. One fear I have that nobody else is aware of is . . .

3. One thing that makes me very sad is . . .

4. One person whom I love dearly is . . .

5. The reason that I love this person is . . .

Reflections on Recovery

Maybe you felt more comfortable expressing your emotions when you were high, sitting around with your using buddies saying, "I love you, man." As your using got out of control, the emotional highs and lows probably became more extreme and more unpredictable. How many times when you were drunk or high did you experience extreme happiness, extreme anger, or extreme sadness? Then, as your brain physically changed to accommodate the drugs, did you notice how you felt when you were not using? Soon, feeling normal was only possible if you put something in your system. It is a powerful cycle that increases as our addiction progresses. Before we know it, we are not even sure what normal is or how it feels.

We can try to ignore our feelings, but it does not change reality: feelings are part of every moment of our lives. Men who are not addicts may be able to survive while suppressing and mislabeling their emotions, but those of us who are addicts risk our sobriety and our lives if we do not grow in emotional awareness.

Use the space below to record any thoughts you have about the material covered in today's session.

Into Action

This optional activity does not have to relate directly to the material covered in this session; however, it should relate in some way to your recovery.

Describe what action step you will take between now and the next session. You also can record what results were achieved.

Recovery Scale

Please take a few moments to mark the degree to which you do each of the following things. You assessed yourself on this scale at the beginning of this module. Please reassess yourself to see where you are now. You will not have to compare your answers with anyone else in the group, nor will you be judged on how well you are doing. This is not a test but an opportunity for you to chart your own progress in recovery. After you finish this scale, go back and look at the one you did earlier.

	Not at All	Just a Little	Pretty Much	Very Much
1. I keep up my physical appearance.				
2. I exercise regularly.				
3. I eat healthy meals.				
4. I get restful sleep.				
5. I regularly go to work/school.				
6. I can adapt to change.				
7. I keep up my living space.				
8. I take constructive criticism well.				
9. I can accept praise.				
10. I laugh at funny things.				
11. I acknowledge my needs and feelings.				
12. I engage in new interests.				
13. I can relax without alcohol or drugs.				
14. I value myself.				

MODULE B

Relationships

Family of Origin

Feeling Okay

Here is a new exercise that you can use to help you to relax or calm yourself and feel more grounded. The "Containment" exercise is designed to help you temporarily set aside some of your issues and concerns. Constantly thinking about certain problems or experiences—especially negative ones—can lead you to use alcohol or other drugs to deal with the stress. This exercise may seem silly at first but, as you become more comfortable with it, you will discover that it is a quick and effective way to reduce your stress and anxiety.

1. In your mind, create a list of all the thoughts and feelings that are bothering you right now. Include any strong negative emotions, thoughts, and memories. For the first couple of times, you can write these down if it is easier for you.
2. Visualize a container of some kind that can hold objects. It could be a box, a trash can, an empty room, or even a hole in the ground.
3. Imagine depositing each of your worries and concerns and bad memories into the container.
4. Place all the distressing items into the container, knowing that it's just for a brief period of time. You can retrieve any and all of these items at any time.
5. Tell yourself that you are now ready to concentrate on the task at hand.

As you practice this, it will get easier, and you will notice that it really does help you to feel more calm and centered. Try it the next time you are feeling distracted and you have a task or activity that requires your full attention.

Family Trees

Most men come into early recovery with long histories of disappointing relationships. Unhealthy relationships feed addictions, and healthy relationships provide the necessary environment for recovery. Your first experience with relationships was with the family you grew up in, which is called your *family of origin*. It is in the family that we first learn powerful messages about relationships. We often re-create relationships in our adult lives that are built on what we learned as children. Many of us did not grow up in healthy families; therefore, we may not know how to create healthy relationships.

The next six sessions focus on relationships and will help you to think about the relationships in your life. The following cartoon, "Family Trees," shows how a family tree typically looked in the 1950s and the very different way one looked in the 1990s and continues to look today. In the 1950s, "family" usually meant two parents and their children. Then those children grew up, married, had their own children, and so on. Today, families are not so neat and tidy. Single mothers and single fathers are raising children, and grandparents are caring for grandchildren. In blended families, children may have two sets of parents, several sets of grandparents, and many stepsisters and stepbrothers. Some kids have same-sex parents or parents who are not married.

Family Trees

1950   1990

Cartoon by Signe Wilkinson. Copyright by Signe Wilkinson, Cartoonists & Writers Syndicate. Reprinted with permission.

Family Roles

Every family is a system of interwoven relationships. In healthy families, these relationships are supportive and empowering and they foster personal growth. In unhealthy families, particularly if abuse or addiction is present, the relationships become unsupportive and disempowering and they limit personal growth. Children who grow up in unhealthy or high-stress families are at high risk of developing problems with addiction.

Research suggests that children in dysfunctional families take on specific roles in order to cope. The four roles are the Hero, the Scapegoat, the Lost Child, and the Mascot. These roles help keep the family system in balance.

Hero. The firstborn child usually becomes the Hero. As the name suggests, the Hero feels a lot of pressure to follow all the rules perfectly and to perform in an outstanding manner. He is expected to represent the family in a positive way. In a high-stress family, the Hero is at risk of becoming overly responsible and needing to be in control at all times.

Scapegoat. The second child often becomes the Scapegoat, the one who continually gets into trouble as a way of getting attention. He is most likely to skip school, steal, and use alcohol or other drugs. As much trouble as this child causes, he relieves stress in the family by taking attention away from the issues between Mom and Dad that aren't being addressed. In a high-stress family, the Scapegoat is at risk of being physically abused.

Lost Child. The third child is likely to become the Lost Child. He can't compete with his older siblings in either positive or negative ways, so he withdraws and isolates himself from the rest of the family. He tends to live in his own world, ignored by his parents and siblings. In a high-stress family, the Lost Child is at risk of being sexually abused or engaging in self-destructive behaviors.

Mascot. The youngest child is frequently the Mascot. He will do almost anything to get attention, and because of his charm and humor, he is often forgiven for any negative behavior. As much trouble as he may cause, his behavior takes the focus off any problems in the family. In a high-stress family, the Mascot is at risk of being physically abused.

These roles are common even in healthy families. The difference is that the less healthy a family is (that is, the more the children are seen as meeting the family's needs, rather than the family meeting the children's needs), the more rigid and pronounced the roles become.

You probably can recognize one role that you played more than any of the others. That was your *primary* role. However, you may also have had a *secondary* role that you took on when a change in the family blocked you from using your primary role. For instance, maybe you were the Hero until one of your younger brothers became a sports star and took over the Hero role, so you shifted into the role of Scapegoat. Or maybe you were sent to a new foster family, where you had to find a new role. In families with fewer than four children, each child may take on multiple roles.

These roles were important to our survival as children, but most of us carry them into adulthood, even though they have outlived some of their usefulness and may have little connection to who we are now.

There are both positive and negative aspects to each of these roles.

Positive and Negative Aspects of Roles

Hero

Positive	*Negative*
independent	fears rejection, confrontation
organized	perfectionist, fears failure
responsible	procrastinates
avoids harmful risk	doesn't get personal needs met
powerful and in control	low self-esteem
focused, attentive	unable to play
loyal	immature "adult-child"
generous with praise	inflexible
successful	unable to label feelings
leader	guilt-ridden
high achiever	feels inadequate
survivor	fears intimacy
motivates self and others	unreasonably high expectations

Scapegoat

Positive

many friends
adapts easily
exciting life
handles stress well
traveler
commands attention
fun loving

Negative

chemically dependent
irresponsible
manipulative
daredevil
passive-aggressive
rationalizes
often on the hot seat
lies, makes up alibis
lacks close connections

Lost Child

Positive

creative, imaginative
well-developed skills, manual dexterity
well-read
good listener, observer
spiritual
resourceful
can work independently
nonconformist
enjoys solitude

Negative

lonely, isolated, withdrawn
lacks social skills
feels invisible, excluded
can be obsessed with self
low self-esteem, distorted self-image
sad, depressed
mistrusts, blames others
fantasizes
inactive, indecisive

Mascot

Positive

sense of humor
charming
joyful
image
eases family tension, keeps the peace
playful, active
attracts attention

Negative

never taken seriously
blames, projects
denies own feelings to maintain

dependent
irresponsible
seeks attention
deflects attention from real problem

From *Leaving the Enchanted Forest: The Path from Relationship Addiction to Intimacy*, by Stephanie Covington and Liana Beckett, 1988. San Francisco: HarperSanFrancisco. Copyright 1988 by Stephanie Covington and Liana Beckett. Reprinted with permission of HarperCollins.

1. What was your primary role in your family? How did you act it out?

2. What was your secondary role? How did you act it out?

3. As you think about your family roles, are there any aspects you would like to leave behind as you move forward in life? If so, what would you like to leave behind?

4. Which of the positive attributes of your roles will be a source of strength for you in recovery?

5. What do you notice about the ways in which your primary family role affects your current relationships?

Assignment

The assignment to be completed before the next session follows:

Refer to pages 66 and 67 (the chart titled "Positive and Negative Aspects of Roles").

1. Review the lists of positive and negative characteristics of your primary role and circle the traits that describe you today.
2. Add any traits that you remember from the session that you do not see on the chart.
3. Then identify one negative aspect of your primary role that you would like to begin working on. Write it in the space below and identify one or two things that you can do immediately that will lessen the negative impact that this has on your life.

Reflections on Recovery

Remembering your family of origin may raise feelings of anger, fear, and pain. This is especially true if you were abused physically, sexually, or psychologically. Your mind may have been flashing back to times when your parents were fighting, when you were yelled at or hit, or when you cried yourself to sleep as a boy. It may be difficult for you to admit that you are having those feelings. When bad feelings from the past are brought up, you can use the breathing and other grounding exercises you have learned to help you become emotionally centered.

Use the space that follows to record any thoughts you have about the material covered in today's session.

Into Action

This is an optional activity. What you choose to do does not necessarily have to relate directly to the material covered in this session; however, it should relate in some way to your recovery.

Some examples are to

1. Ask one (or both) of your parents, or an older family member, about your grandparents and their ancestors, and start to map out a "family tree."
2. Identify one of the positive aspects of your primary role and then make specific notes about the times that this attribute has helped you in life.

Use the space below to describe what action step you will take between now and the next session. You also can record what results were achieved.

Recovery Scale

Please take a few moments to mark the degree to which you do each of the things listed below. You can make an "X" or a circle on each line as your response.

You will complete this form again at the end of this module on Relationships to see how you have changed. You will not have to compare your answers with anyone else in the group, nor will you be judged on how well you are doing. This is not a test but an opportunity for you to chart your own progress in recovery.

	Not at All	Just a Little	Pretty Much	Very Much
1. I share my needs and wants with others.				
2. I socialize with others.				
3. I stay connected to friends and loved ones.				
4. I nurture my loved ones.				
5. I am straightforward with others.				
6. I can tell the difference between supportive and unsupportive relationships.				
7. I have developed a support system.				
8. I offer support to others.				
9. I participate in conversations with my family members, friends, and/or co-workers.				
10. I listen to and respect others.				
11. I have clean and sober friends.				
12. I can be trusted.				

Barriers to Relationships

The Issues of Abuse, Trauma, Power, and Control

Domestic violence is defined as "any exploitive or threatening behaviors intended to harm or exert power over another family or household member."

Abuse in the Family

In the previous session, you learned some of the ways in which interactions among family members can have long-lasting effects on every facet of your life. In high-stress families, there is a risk that the children will be abused. If parents use alcohol or other drugs, the risk is higher. Many children do not know that they have been abused because they assume that the behavior in their family is normal. Following are examples of types of abuse.

> **Physical abuse.** Examples of physical abuse are pinching, slapping, pushing, hair pulling, spitting, restraining, shaking, kicking, choking, dragging, ripping clothing, biting, throwing objects, hitting with objects, punching, burning, and stabbing.
>
> **Sexual abuse.** Examples of sexual abuse are telling sexual jokes, harassment, violating another's boundaries, giving inappropriate information, inappropriate touching, voyeurism, sexual hugs, commenting about developing bodies, reading or viewing pornography with a child, exhibitionism, fondling, French-kissing a child, oral sex, and penetration.

75

Emotional abuse. Examples of emotional abuse are silence, withdrawing, with-holding approval or affection, manipulation through dishonesty, intimidation, and not acknowledging the other person's feelings.

Verbal abuse. Examples of verbal abuse are name-calling, ridicule, constant criticism, blaming, threatening, and shouting or screaming.

Some lasting effects of abuse are powerlessness, numbness, rage, hatred, shame, fear, mistrust, confusion, poor self-esteem, poor judgment, antisocial behavior, fear of intimacy, oversexualized behavior, and an inability to have healthy sexual relationships. In addition, children raised in abusive homes are at high risk of becoming addicted to alcohol and other drugs, and men who are victims of abuse are at risk of becoming abusers.

Acknowledging abuse can be difficult for men if they associate it with admitting weakness. As a result, many men keep their histories of abuse hidden, from themselves as well as others, in order to feel strong and in control of their lives. It is important to know that if you were abused as a boy, it was wrong and it wasn't your fault. No matter what you did and what others have told you, it was inexcusable.

Trauma

Trauma is any stressor that occurs in a sudden and forceful way and is experienced as overwhelming. Men who have experienced traumatic events describe feelings of intense fear, helplessness, and horror. These are normal reactions to abnormal or extreme situations.

No two people experience trauma in the same way. What may be a traumatic event for one person may not be for another. Sometimes, trauma has occurred but may not be recognized immediately because the person may see violent or abusive events as normal.

There are many forms of trauma: emotional, sexual, and physical abuse; catastrophic injury and illness; the loss of a loved one; an accident; abandonment; witnessing violence; a natural disaster; combat; kidnapping; torture; and so on.

A *trigger* is something that sets off a physical or emotional reaction in a traumatized person. This could be a smell, a sound, a physical setting, or something else that reminds the person of the traumatic event.

The effects of trauma often result in something called post-traumatic stress disorder (PTSD). The American Psychiatric Association identifies three categories of PTSD symptoms:

A Man's Workbook

Reexperiencing includes disturbed sleep, intrusive memories, distressing dreams, nightmares, flashbacks, reliving the event, and viewing the world as unsafe.

Numbing and avoidance includes mistrust of others, isolation and disconnection, emotional or psychic numbness, low self-esteem, neglect of health, dissociation, ability to remember memories or feelings but not both, memory loss for certain events, and loss of faith and hope.

Hyperarousal includes intense emotions, difficulty sleeping, panic and anxiousness, self-harm, risky behaviors, irritability, anger, and difficulty concentrating.

If you have been traumatized, you may recognize some of these symptoms. Unresolved trauma can affect your physical health, your emotional well-being, your ability to develop and maintain healthy relationships, and your sexual health. You may be comforted to know that there is a name for what you are experiencing, that you are not alone, and that there are people who understand and can help. Part of the process of healing from trauma, like recovering from addiction, is developing connection and support with others.

Power and Control

In our society, men tend to have more power than women and certainly have more power than children. Some men use that power in abusive ways to control situations and other people. Many men need to take a very honest look at how they have been abusive to others. Some degree of abusiveness seems to be tolerated in some people's concept of masculinity. You may act abusively or violently in the moment because you are overwhelmed with emotion or acting out of a traumatic trigger. However, abusive behavior is never appropriate or justifiable. Abusive behavior is damaging to both the victim and the perpetrator.

The figure that follows is the Power and Control Wheel. There are twelve ways that one person can be abusive to another.

The Power and Control Wheel

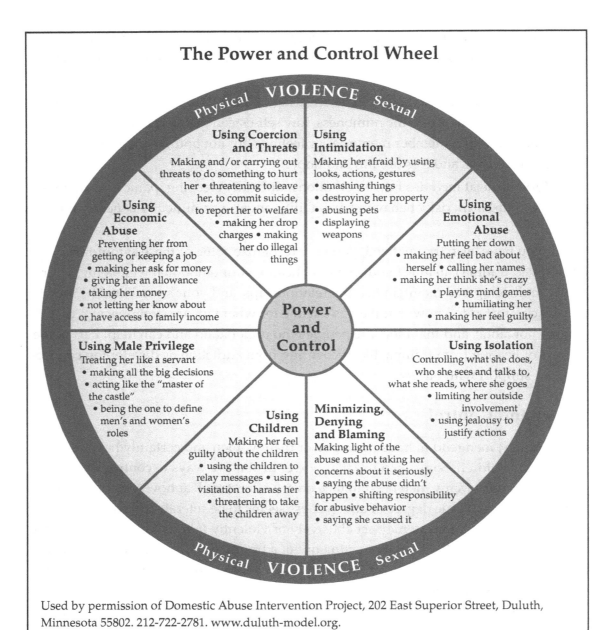

VIOLENCE Physical Sexual

Power and Control

Using Coercion and Threats
Making and/or carrying out threats to do something to hurt her • threatening to leave her, to commit suicide, to report her to welfare • making her drop charges • making her do illegal things

Using Intimidation
Making her afraid by using looks, actions, gestures • smashing things • destroying her property • abusing pets • displaying weapons

Using Economic Abuse
Preventing her from getting or keeping a job • making her ask for money • giving her an allowance • taking her money • not letting her know about or have access to family income

Using Emotional Abuse
Putting her down • making her feel bad about herself • calling her names • making her think she's crazy • playing mind games • humiliating her • making her feel guilty

Using Male Privilege
Treating her like a servant • making all the big decisions • acting like the "master of the castle" • being the one to define men's and women's roles

Using Isolation
Controlling what she does, who she sees and talks to, what she reads, where she goes • limiting her outside involvement • using jealousy to justify actions

Using Children
Making her feel guilty about the children • using the children to relay messages • using visitation to harass her • threatening to take the children away

Minimizing, Denying and Blaming
Making light of the abuse and not taking her concerns about it seriously • saying the abuse didn't happen • shifting responsibility for abusive behavior • saying she caused it

VIOLENCE Physical Sexual

Used by permission of Domestic Abuse Intervention Project, 202 East Superior Street, Duluth, Minnesota 55802. 212-722-2781. www.duluth-model.org.

In the spaces provided, try to give a specific example of how you have used each of these behaviors to control another person or a situation. There may be some forms of power and control that you have never used. Leave those spaces blank.

Emotional abuse

Physical abuse

Economic abuse

Sexual abuse

Coercion and threats

Intimidation

A Man's Workbook

Isolation

Using children

Using male privilege

Minimizing

Denying

Blaming

A Place of Peace

Here is another grounding exercise for you to use when you feel emotionally distressed. Taking a few minutes each day to relax and find some peace is an effective way to stay emotionally centered.

Close your eyes or, if you don't feel comfortable doing that, lower your eyelids.

1. Start by breathing. Take a deep breath in while you silently count to four.
2. Now breathe out slowly while you silently count to four.
3. Remember to breathe from your abdomen. Breathe in again for a count of four.
4. Breathe out again to a count of four.
5. Now picture in your mind a place of peace. Maybe you have been there before or maybe it is a place of your dreams. Maybe it's your bed or a comfortable chair. Maybe it's sitting by a lake or lying in the sun at the ocean. Maybe it's a special place you visited as a child or a scene from one of your favorite movies. It may be a real place or an imaginary place. See that place in your mind.
6. Keep breathing slowly and deeply.
7. Let the muscles in your face relax.
8. Let your brow relax.
9. Let your jaw relax.
10. Let your neck and your shoulders relax.
11. Imagine all the tension draining out of them. Let it go.
12. Let your hands and arms go limp next to you.
13. Let your middle relax—your chest and your abdomen.
14. Keep breathing in and out.
15. Let your hips and your legs relax.
16. Let your feet relax.
17. Relax your whole body and imagine yourself in that favorite, safe place. This is your place of peace. You are safe in this place. Your life is the life you always wanted it to be. You are sober. You are a loving and caring man who is committed to being of service to others.
18. Feel the peace.
19. As you breathe in these next couple of times, breathe in the word "Peace."

20. As you breathe out, exhale all the pain from your past and all the negative feelings and thoughts.

21. Breathe in peace.

22. Breathe out pain.

23. Now open your eyes and slowly return to the present.

Assignment

The assignment to be completed before the next session follows:

Answer the following two questions in the spaces provided.

1. What are some examples of how we can use control or personal power in positive ways?

2. Can you provide any examples from your recovery of where you can already see yourself using control and power differently—in a more positive way? What are these examples?

Reflections on Recovery

In this session, you looked at the harmful consequences that occur when men attempt to exert power and control over others. However, exercising control over your own behaviors can be a very healthy practice. Power and control are not intrinsically bad; it is just that a lot of us use them inappropriately. Recovery is practically impossible if you do not learn how to exercise your personal power and self-control. Your personal power is what enables you to call someone for help despite your fear and shame. Your personal power is what allows you to learn how to stand up for yourself in healthy ways, set boundaries, and deal effectively with conflict.

Use the space that follows to record any thoughts you have about the material covered in today's session.

Into Action

This is an optional activity. What you choose to do does not necessarily have to relate directly to the material covered in this session; however, it should relate in some way to your recovery.

Use the space below to describe what action step you will take between now and the next session. You also can record what results were achieved.

Fathers

Fathers and Sons

Over the last several sessions, you have begun to look at your self-identity, your feelings, and your relationships. One thing that all these issues have in common is how they tend to stem from our relationships with our fathers. A lot of us learned what to think about our feelings and how to express them from our fathers. In watching our fathers and the other men in our lives, we learned how to be men.

All of us have had the experience of being sons. Even if you were not raised by your biological father, there probably was some man in your life who played the father role—perhaps your grandfather or an adoptive father or a foster father. You may have felt close to the man who fathered you or you may have felt distant from him. You may have felt many emotions about him, including love, pride, anger, resentment, and sadness. Maybe your emotions have changed as you have grown up. No matter what our fathers did or did not do, we often have strong feelings about them. Even as adults, we often still carry feelings about what we wish our fathers were like.

Take some time to answer the following questions as honestly as you can.

1. Think back to when you were a child under the age of twelve. What was your relationship with your father—or the person who was substituting in the role of your father—like at that time?

2. What was your relationship with your father or father substitute like when you were a teenager?

A Man's Workbook

3. If your father is still alive, how would you describe your relationship with him now?

4. What do you know about your father's life when he was a child, a teenager, and an adult? To your knowledge, was he ever rebellious or unhappy in his role as a man and husband? What did he do about it?

5. Do you believe that your father was able to achieve the goals he had set for himself? What were some of these?

6. Did your father have a problem with alcohol or other drugs? If so, discuss some specific ways in which you were affected by this.

A Man's Workbook

7. What did you learn about being a man from your father?

8. In what ways do you think that your father is, or would be, disappointed in the man that you have become?

9. In what ways do you think that your father is, or would be, proud of the man you have become?

Father Myths

Boys typically grow up idealizing their fathers. When you were very young, you probably saw your father as a powerful figure and larger than life. His approval may have been the most important thing in the world to you. As you got older, especially if there was abuse, neglect, or addiction in the family, you may have come to resent and even fear him. It is important to recognize that, like us, our fathers were full of healthy qualities and unhealthy qualities, strengths and weaknesses, needs and desires. It is important for you to remember that your father was once a boy and a teenager just as you were.

Answer the following questions in the spaces provided.

1. What are the things we've been told that fathers are supposed to do? What are our expectations of them?

2. How do men feel when they are expected to nurture and show affection for their children?

3. How do children feel when their fathers only do the "typical" things and are not engaged emotionally in their children's lives?

4. What happens when Dad is an addict and doesn't do even the things on the list?

5. What do you think boy and girl children get angry at their fathers for?

6. What message are we sending to children about what they should expect from a father?

7. For those of you who are fathers, what did you expect to feel when you had children?

8. What did you actually feel?

9. Did you have an idea of how you wanted to be as a father?

10. How hard has it been to be the father you wanted to be?

Assignment

The assignment to be completed before the next session follows:

Write a letter to your father. You won't mail this letter and you do not have to share it with him, but it will be a chance for you to put on paper what you've always wanted to tell him. Take some time to think about what you'd really like to say. If you had a stepfather or grandfather who was the primary male figure in your life, and you would prefer to write a letter to him, that is fine.

Spelling and grammar don't count; just write what comes out of your heart. Try to say the things that you always wanted to say but were never able to.

If you are genuinely uncomfortable with your writing abilities, you may create drawings that reflect what you want to say, or create a poem or rap, or share a song that expresses what you would like to communicate.

Thinking about and talking to either of our parents can raise some powerful emotions, both positive and negative. Looking at painful issues can help us gain the power to make better choices in the future. Think about the last session, when we explored some of the barriers to healthy relationships. Making peace with our parents can help us to find peace and make healthier choices in our current relationships.

It also is important to honor the gifts that your father has given you and to express your feelings of love and gratitude. If your father is no longer living, you may want to describe your feelings of grief and loss.

You may use the space provided in this workbook to write or draw your message to your father. If you prefer, or if you think that you will need more space, do your writing or drawing on a separate piece of paper.

You may choose to share this letter with your father; however, carefully consider whether you and he are ready to have this experience.

Dear

Visualization Exercise

You may have recalled some painful memories and expressed some equally painful feelings when writing the letter to your father. Hopefully, you were able to recall some happy memories as well. This exercise will help you to focus on positive and healing thoughts.

This brief grounding exercise involves some visualization. You will be slowly taking in a deep breath and then letting it out. As you draw your breath in, imagine all the peaceful and joyful times you had with your father. As you breathe out, expel any of the pain you feel about your father, particularly any of the bad feelings or memories that came up today.

1. Breathe in slowly. Envision the good times you've had with your father. You may even want to smile.
2. Now breathe out slowly. Release any pain you carry from your relationship with your father. You may want to make a sound as you release it.
3. Breathe in. Envision the good times with your father.
4. Breathe out and release the negative.
5. Repeat this two more times.

Reflections on Recovery

Two sessions ago, we discussed how limiting our roles as children often were. The roles of father and mother also can be limiting. It can be hard for children to think of their fathers and mothers as people. As an adult, when you begin to see your parents as human, you can begin to deal with your feelings about them. Understanding your father as a man can help you to appreciate your own masculinity. For example, if you are angry with your father, you may tend to have conflict with other men, especially those who remind you of your father. You may have a hard time trusting them as a result of how your father treated you when you were a child.

Use the space below to record any thoughts you have about the material covered in today's session.

Into Action

This is an optional activity. What you choose to do does not necessarily have to relate directly to the material covered in this session; however, it should relate in some way to your recovery.

Use the space below to describe what action step you will take between now and the next session. You also can record what results were achieved.

Mothers

Mothers and Sons

Mothers do the majority of the child rearing in most families. Regardless of the relationship you had with your father, your mother likely was the constant in your life. That is what mothers are expected to do. You may have been taught what to *think* about your feelings by your father, but your mother showed you what it is like to be cared for, so she helped you to *experience* feelings. How your father or the other men in your life treated your mother, and how you may have perceived your mother allowing herself to be treated, affected how you thought of your mother. More important, it affects how you think of women in general and how you treat women.

Take some time to answer the following questions as honestly as you can.

1. Think back to when you were a child under the age of twelve. What was your relationship with your mother—or the person who played the role of your mother—like at that time?

2. What was your relationship with your mother like when you were a teenager?

A Man's Workbook

3. If your mother is still alive, how would you describe your relationship with her now?

4. What do you know about your mother's life when she was a child, a teenager, and an adult? To your knowledge, was she ever rebellious or unhappy in her roles as a woman and wife? What did she do about this?

5. Do you believe that your mother was able to achieve the goals she set for herself? What were some of them?

6. Did your mother ever have a problem with alcohol or other drugs? If so, discuss some specific ways in which you were affected by this.

7. What did you learn about being a man from your mother?

8. How did your father or other men treat your mother?

9. In what ways do you think that your mother is, or would be, disappointed in the man that you have become?

10. In what ways do you think that your mother is, or would be, proud of the man you have become?

Mother Myths

You may have difficulty communicating anything negative about your mother. Mothers are supposed to be always loving, protective, supportive, and generous to their children. Sons are supposed to regard their mothers with total respect, affection, and dedication. You may perceive any anger or other negative emotion that you feel toward your mother as a betrayal. But it is important to take the time to think about your mother as a real, three-dimensional person, with good and bad qualities, just as you did with your father. When you are able to see your mother as a person in her own right, you will be better able to come to terms with your relationship with her. You may also develop more realistic expectations of the other women in your life.

Answer the following questions in the spaces provided.

1. What does society say that mothers are supposed to do? What do we expect mothers to do? (The list of expectations of mothers usually is longer than the list of expectations of fathers. We seem to expect more from mothers.)

2. Why isn't it possible for a woman to do all the things that are expected of mothers?

3. What happens when Mom is an addict and doesn't do even the things on the list?

110   *A Man's Workbook*

4. It's common for both boy and girl children to be very angry at their mothers for what their mothers did not do or for the caretaking they did not get, but not for them to be as mad at their fathers for what *they* failed to do. Why do you suppose this is? (This often is the reason that adult men are angry at women; they feel that their women partners should make up for what their mothers didn't give them.)

5. What message are we sending to children about what they should expect from a mother?

6. Review your answer to question 8 on page 107 about how your mother was treated by your father or other men.

7. How did that feel when you were a child? What message do you think it sent to you about women?

A Man's Workbook

Assignment

The assignment to be completed before the next session follows:

> Write a letter to your mother. You won't mail this letter and you do not have to share it with her, but it will be a chance for you to put on paper what you've always wanted to tell her. Take some time to think about what you'd really like to say. If you had a stepmother or grandmother who was the primary female figure in your life, and you would prefer to write a letter to her, that is fine.
>
> Spelling and grammar don't count; just write what comes out of your heart. Try to say the things that you always wanted to say but were never able to.
>
> If you are genuinely uncomfortable with your writing abilities, you may create drawings that reflect what you want to say, or create a poem or rap, or share a song that expresses what you would like to communicate.

Thinking about and talking to either of our parents can raise some powerful emotions, both positive and negative. Looking at painful issues can help us gain the power to make better choices in the future. Making peace with our parents can help us to find peace and make healthier choices in our current relationships.

It also is important to honor the gifts that your mother has given you and to express your feelings of love and gratitude. If your mother is no longer living, you may want to describe your feelings of grief and loss.

You may use the space provided in this workbook to write or draw your message to your mother. If you prefer, or if you think that you will need more space, do your writing or drawing on a separate piece of paper.

You may choose to share this letter with your mother; however, carefully consider whether you and she are ready to have this experience.

Dear

Visualization Exercise

You may have recalled some painful memories and expressed some equally painful feelings when writing the letter to your mother. Hopefully, you were able to recall some happy memories as well. This next exercise will help you to focus on positive and healing thoughts.

This is very similar to the exercise from the last session. You'll be slowly taking a deep breath and then letting it out. As you draw your breath in, imagine all the peaceful and joyful times you had with your mother. As you breathe out, expel any of the pain you feel about your mother, particularly any of the feelings or memories that came up today.

1. Breathe in slowly. Envision the good times you've had with your mother. You may even want to smile.
2. Now breathe out slowly. Release any pain you carry from your relationship with your mother. You may want to make a sound as you release it.
3. Breathe in and envision the good times with your mother.
4. Breathe out and release the negative.
5. Repeat this two more times.

Reflections on Recovery

Understanding our mothers as women can help us to better understand how we relate to and treat other women in our lives. It also can help us to honor the parts of us that often are described as "feminine": our sensitivity, our compassion, our creativity, our gentleness, and our caring for others. If we are angry with our mothers, we may tend to treat women badly, especially those who remind us of our mothers.

Use the space below to record any thoughts you have about the material covered in today's session.

Into Action

This is an optional activity. What you choose to do does not necessarily have to relate directly to the material covered in this session; however, it should relate in some way to your recovery.

Use the space below to describe what action step you will take between now and the next session. You also can record what results were achieved.

Creating Healthy Relationships and Support Systems

Growth-Fostering Relationships

Sessions 6 and 7 emphasized your relationships with your mother and father, because those probably are the ones that have had the greatest influence on how you relate to people today. However, other relationships are also extremely important: those with your spouse or partner, your friends, your teammates, and your co-workers. Some of these relationships undoubtedly have been healthy and supportive, and some probably have been unhealthy and unsupportive.

If you haven't had many supportive relationships in your life, you may not know what to expect from one. A supportive relationship should help you to grow. Recovery is growth. Addiction is a downward spiral and, as your addiction takes over your life, your relationships follow you down in that spiral. You push away the healthier people in your life or they leave. The relationships that are associated with addiction tend to be unhealthy. You are not likely to grow in those relationships, and they are never as important as the addiction.

Unhealthy, unsupportive relationships produce

- Diminished zest or vitality
- Disempowerment
- Confusion, lack of clarity
- A diminished sense of self-worth
- A turning away from relationships

117

In healthy and supportive relationships, each person

- Feels a greater sense of zest (vitality, energy)
- Feels more able to act and does act
- Has a more accurate perception of himself or herself and the other person(s)
- Feels a greater sense of self-worth
- Feels more connected to the other person(s) and feels a greater motivation for connections with other people beyond those in the specific relationship

Many things can give support. Emotional support when you're going through a hard time can be in the form of someone who really listens to you without giving advice and trying to fix you. When you are living in the free world and someone gives you a ride to work or an A.A. meeting they are giving practical support. Someone might support you by checking in with you every day to see how you're doing in your recovery and patting you on the back because you've had another day sober.

Developing and maintaining supportive relationships sometimes can be difficult for men. You may believe that asking for support or help is "unmanly" or an admission of weakness or failure.

Answer the following questions in the spaces provided:

1. You've been in this program for ten sessions now. What are some ways in which you've felt supported here?

2. Of the various kinds of support you've had in your life, what has been especially helpful?

3. In what areas of your life have you felt the most comfortable asking for support? Why is this?

4. Think of a time when you were in crisis or having a hard time and you enlisted the support of someone else. What was that like?

Relationship Maps

We all need people in our lives to provide emotional and practical support. We need people who will support our recovery. Supportive relationships will help you achieve

- Growth
- Energy
- Empowerment
- Knowledge
- Self-worth
- Connections

In contrast, with unsupportive, unhealthy, or abusive relationships, you will feel

- Drained of energy
- Disempowered
- Confused
- Worthless
- Isolated

The first illustration that follows is a sample of a Relationship Map. It shows one man's relationship to people in his past and present, as well as his plans for relationships in the future. You will create your own map on the page that follows it.

- Put yourself in the middle of the page in a circle.
- Then add the relationships in your life.
- Draw circles for individuals and draw squares for groups.

Perhaps each of your parents, your friend, your girlfriend, and each of your children is in a circle as a present relationship. Your ex-partner is entered as a past relationship. If you are doing this program as part of a group, the group will be a present relationship in a square. If you are in Alcoholics Anonymous (A.A.), Narcotics Anonymous (N.A.), or Gamblers Anonymous (G.A.) now, put that group in a square in the present. If you are not yet going to Twelve Step meetings, you might put a square for one in the future section of your map, if that's a source of support you want to add.

Then notice the different kinds of lines that connect the self to the other individuals and groups. A solid line shows that this is a relationship you already have that you want to maintain. A dotted line with an arrow toward the other is a relationship that you want to start. Maybe you are not already going to A.A. but want to start. So there's a dotted line with an arrow. A solid line with slash marks through it shows that this is a relationship you want to end. Maybe your best friends currently are all alcoholics or drug addicts. They've been drinking or using buddies, but they aren't going to be good support for you in recovery, so maybe you'll decide that you want to end those relationships. That's why some of the lines on the sample have slash marks through them.

As you create your map, think about the qualities of healthy and unhealthy relationships.

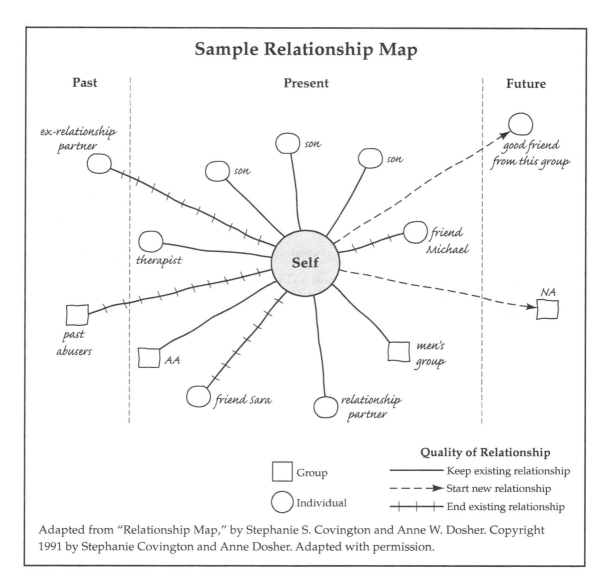

Sample Relationship Map

Adapted from "Relationship Map," by Stephanie S. Covington and Anne W. Dosher. Copyright 1991 by Stephanie Covington and Anne Dosher. Adapted with permission.

Relationship Map

Past | Present | Future

Self

Group

Individual

Quality of Relationship

———— Keep existing relationship

– – – ▶ Start new relationship

+——+——+ End existing relationship

Adapted from "Relationship Map," by Stephanie S. Covington and Anne W. Dosher. Copyright 1991 by Stephanie Covington and Anne Dosher. Adapted with permission.

Answer the following questions in the spaces provided.

1. As you look to the future, which of your current relationships do you want to continue and strengthen?

2. Which of your current relationships do you need to end because they will not support your recovery and help you grow?

3. What new, supportive relationships do you want to pursue?

4. You have relationships not just with your family and friends but also with the community and nation in which you live, and you have the power to make a difference in all those relationships. What kind of changes in your community or country would you like to work toward in the future? What could you do as one step toward making a difference in the area you choose?

Twelve Step Meetings

Twelve Step meetings, such as those presented by A.A., N.A., or G.A., are places where you can begin to develop supportive relationships. What is great about these meetings is that men are expected to connect with others, get support, and be "a part of." You will not be teased or put down for admitting that you need help, feel scared and confused, or are simply struggling in your addiction. It will be much easier for you to stay in recovery when you are in a culture that embraces, encourages, and even expects supportive relationships.

Assignment

The assignments to be completed before the next session follow:

Put some additional effort into completing your Relationship Map. Also, answer the questions on pages 123 and 124. You will have a few minutes to complete your map and then review it at the beginning of the next session.

Ask someone for help in an area that will strengthen the support you have for recovery. Examples are asking a family member or friend for help with a situation that you are struggling with; asking someone at a Twelve Step meeting to be your sponsor and setting up a time to meet with him; and explaining to an old, using friend the new rules about alcohol or drug use that you have established for yourself.

Reflections on Recovery

The consistent theme of the last five sessions is understanding how important it is to develop and maintain healthy relationships. We talk in recovery about changing our playmates and our playgrounds. You may have interpreted that to mean that you need to end every relationship with people who use alcohol or other drugs. This is not necessarily so.

However, you do need to learn how to set boundaries with people. You need to be very direct with them about the new "rules" or boundaries you have established for yourself. The new rules dictate that sobriety is the highest priority in your life. When you enforce your boundaries, some of your family members, or friends, or even your partner may not respect your wishes. When your friends and family members do respect these new boundaries, you will know that there is more to the relationship than just using together, and that becomes something to build on. If you currently are in jail or prison, it will be very important to let your family members and friends know about the new rules before you are released from custody. You also need to think about which people you will absolutely have to avoid.

Use the space below to record any thoughts you have about the material covered in today's session.

Into Action

This is an optional activity. What you choose to do does not necessarily have to relate directly to the material covered in this session; however, it should relate in some way to your recovery.

Use the space below to describe what action step you will take between now and the next session. You also can record what results were achieved.

Effective Communication and Intimacy

Communication and Conflict

All humans have basic wants and needs in relationships. We want to be understood, appreciated, cared for, and supported. We need compassion, empathy, affection, physical contact, and cooperation. Asking for these things from your family members, friends, partners, and co-workers is not always easy. As you grew up, you may not have learned how to effectively communicate these wants and needs.

Furthermore, conflict is an inevitable part of any human relationship. No two people are going to agree on everything all the time. How you handle conflict has a large effect on the quality of your relationships. Learning how to handle conflict effectively also may help to keep you out of trouble in the future.

There are four basic styles of communication and conflict resolution:

Passive. A passive response to a situation is to do nothing or to agree to do something that you really don't want to do. You may believe that you are being treated unfairly yet decide not to say anything. Passive behavior is a problematic form of communication because there is no "self" in it. Passive communicators seek to avoid conflict at all costs. You give up your wants and needs in order to temporarily keep the peace.

Passive-aggressive. A passive-aggressive response can be the most confusing form of communication. You might verbally agree to a request but intend to do something entirely different. An example is agreeing to work overtime, even if you don't want to and think that it is an unreasonable request. Then you show

129

up late or call in sick or perform the job poorly. This is an indirect way of showing anger and controlling situations without taking responsibility for your true feelings.

Aggressive. This can be a dangerous form of communication. There is too much "self" in this style. Aggressive communicators are going to be "right" and get their way at all costs. Aggressiveness can take the form of interrupting, yelling, blaming, threatening, and even violence. Aggression frequently is rewarded in the short term, because other people become afraid and back down. You might get what you want, but there is a considerable cost to the relationship. Aggression also can lead to legal problems.

Assertive. This form of communication should be your goal. When you practice assertiveness, you are clearly stating what you want and need. Assertive communicators respect their own needs and boundaries and those of other people. This is the form of communication that is least emotion driven, most honest, and most effective in the long term.

Consider this situation:

> You have made plans to go to a ballgame with your two best friends and already have purchased the tickets. You informed your partner about these plans several weeks ago and you are eagerly looking forward to the day. It is the night before the game, and your partner tells you that she has invited family members over for a cookout and is counting on your being present. She says that you never told her about your plans. She asks you to cancel your plans with your friends.

1. Describe a passive response to this situation. What would you say and do? How would you feel afterward? How might your partner feel?

2. Describe a passive-aggressive response to this situation. What would you say and do? How would you feel afterward? How might your partner feel?

3. Describe an aggressive response to this situation. What would you say and do? How would you feel afterward? How might your partner feel?

4. Describe an assertive response to this situation. What would you say and do? How would you feel afterward? How might your partner feel?

A Man's Workbook

Each style of communication and conflict resolution has some "payoffs" (advantages) and some "costs" (disadvantages). List as many as you can think of in the spaces that follow.

Passive

Payoffs   Costs

Passive-Aggressive

Payoffs   Costs

Aggressive

Payoffs   Costs

Intimacy

Intimacy is defined as an emotional experience of connection with another person. These are some of the characteristics of intimacy:

- An expression of feelings in an atmosphere of little or no threat
- Teaching you about me while I'm also learning about you
- Sharing thoughts and feelings with each other in a respectful way—each of us being open and vulnerable
- Love, mutuality, and compassion built on a foundation of respect

Intimacy may or may not involve physical contact or sexual activity. Many of us were raised to believe that intimacy and sex are basically the same thing. Sex may be an aspect of an intimate relationship, but there are many different types of intimacy. In fact, you probably have quite a few intimate relationships in your life. Each of these offers you connection and support.

Types of Intimacy

Sexual. Sharing physical and sensual pleasure

Emotional. Awareness and sharing of significant thoughts and feelings

Intellectual. Sharing the world of ideas; having mutual respect for intellectual capacities

Recreational. Sharing experiences of sports, hobbies, travel, and other fun

Work. Sharing common tasks; supporting each other in responsibilities

Spiritual. Sharing philosophies, religious experiences, and the "meaning of life"

Creative. Being co-creators of a project; helping each other to grow

Crisis. Sharing closeness in coping with tragedy, problems, or pain

Conflict. Facing and struggling together with differences

Communication. Being honest, open, and trusting; engaging in positive confrontation

Commitment. Deriving togetherness from dedication to a common cause

Aesthetic. Sharing experiences of beauty, art, music, theater, dance, and so forth

From *The Intimate Marriage,* by Howard J. Clinebell and Charlotte H. Clinebell, 1970. New York: Harper & Row. Copyright 1970 by Howard J. Clinebell and Charlotte H. Clinebell. Adapted with permission.

Assignment

The assignment to be completed before the next session follows:

Review the different types of intimate relationships on the previous page. For each type of intimacy, list two or three significant people with whom you have that kind of relationship. There may be a few categories for which you can't identify anyone. That's okay; we don't all have every type of intimate relationship in our lives at all times.

Sexual

Emotional

Intellectual

Recreational

Work

Spiritual

Creative

Crisis

Conflict

Communication

Commitment

Aesthetic

Reflections on Recovery

Over the last six sessions, you have considered your relationships and your ability to have relationships in new ways. You started by looking at your family of origin and the roles that you learned growing up. You learned how men often are trained to end up in unhealthy relationships. You explored the issues of power and control and how they may get in the way of your achieving what you want in your relationships. You analyzed your relationships with your father and mother. You learned how important it is to develop healthy, supportive relationships that will help you grow as a man. Finally, you looked at ways to maintain and improve your supportive relationships.

Use the space below to record any thoughts you have about the material covered in today's session.

Into Action

For this optional activity, what you choose to do does not have to relate directly to the material covered in this session; however, it should relate in some way to your recovery.

Use the space below to describe what action step you will take between now and the next session. You also can record what results were achieved.

Recovery Scale

Please take a few moments to mark the degree to which you do each of the things on the scale. You assessed yourself on this scale at the beginning of this module. Please reassess yourself to see where you are now. Your answers will not be compared with those of anyone else and you will not be judged on how well you are doing. This is not a test but an opportunity for you to chart your own progress in recovery. After you finish this scale, go back and look at the one you completed earlier.

	Not at All	Just a Little	Pretty Much	Very Much
1. I share my needs and wants with others.				
2. I socialize with others.				
3. I stay connected to friends and loved ones.				
4. I nurture my loved ones.				
5. I am straightforward with others.				
6. I can tell the difference between supportive and unsupportive relationships.				
7. I have developed a support system.				
8. I offer support to others.				
9. I participate in conversations with my family members, friends, and/or co-workers.				
10. I listen to and respect others.				
11. I have clean and sober friends.				
12. I can be trusted.				

MODULE C

Sexuality

Sexuality and Addiction

Feeling Okay

Here is another grounding exercise that you can use to help center yourself and to focus on positive thoughts and emotions. Sit in a comfortable position with your feet on the floor. Concentrate on your breathing. Feel your body expand from the center and release back toward the center.

With each breath, breathe a little deeper, moving further down into your abdomen.

As you breathe in, visualize taking in positive things, such as self-love, hope, courage, and joy. As you breathe out, visualize expelling the negative things that you don't want in your life, such as self-criticism, despair, anger, stress, and fear. Do this for approximately two minutes.

Practice this exercise at home, school, or work. You will find that you can quickly and easily move from a stressful state to one of positive energy.

Talking About Sex

Most of us have never had a thorough education on human sexuality, even though it is one of the most basic elements of who we are. Most people feel uncomfortable asking questions about sexual matters. In our society, open and honest discussion about sex is frequently discouraged. You have probably heard all kinds of confusing and even contradictory messages about what is okay to discuss and what isn't. During the sessions in this module of the *Helping Men Recover* program, you will have the opportunity to ask any questions about sex. Your facilitator-counselor will show you where a Question Box will be kept so that you can submit written questions—anonymously if you wish.

We'll start with a definition of sexuality. Sexuality is much more than sexual behavior. It is an identification, a biological drive, an orientation, and an outlook. Sexuality involves our physical, emotional, social, and spiritual selves. Even if you are in jail or prison, you are constantly dealing with your sexuality. One definition of healthy adult sexuality is "the physical, emotional, social, and spiritual parts of ourselves integrated into our identities and ways of living." Your sexuality includes your perceptions and feelings about yourself as a man and your perceptions and feelings about others. It involves how you act and with whom you act. So sexuality is not just about having sex; it involves many aspects of who you are.

Addiction affects you physically, emotionally, socially, and spiritually, so it's not surprising that addiction also affects every area of your sexuality. Addressing and healing all aspects of your sexuality is an important part of your recovery process. You may think that it isn't manly to admit that you don't have all the answers or that you experience any feelings of insecurity, fear, or shame regarding sex and sexuality. However, becoming comfortable with your sexuality and coming to terms with your sexual past is essential to your well-being and to your recovery.

Answer the following questions in the spaces provided. For the third question, answer Question 3a if you are living at home, and answer Question 3b if you are living in a jail or prison.

1. How did you first learn about sex?

2. What are your earliest memories of being sexually aware or sexually aroused?

3a. Who can you talk to about sex in an open and honest manner?

3b. What are your concerns about your sexual self while you are in custody?

4. How does it feel to talk about sex with other men in this setting?

5. What are your concerns about being sexual as a clean and sober man?

Sexual Functioning

For many addicted men, there is a high correlation between sexual behavior and the use of mood-altering chemicals. You may have used alcohol or other drugs to overcome shyness or fear of rejection in seeking sexual partners. You may have used in an effort to enhance your sexual performance. You might have engaged in sexual behavior that violated your value system while under the influence. You may have used alcohol or other drugs to deal with feelings of shame or guilt resulting from sexual experiences. You may not have had any sexual experiences without the use of alcohol or drugs, and you may be concerned about what sex will be like when you are in recovery.

One of the most common myths that men believe is that using alcohol and other drugs will improve their sex lives. You may have felt more attractive and more confident while under the influence. You may have felt that being high improved your sexual performance. In fact, most mood-altering chemicals have long-term, negative effects on sexuality and sexual performance.

Alcohol. Alcohol use generally lowers inhibitions, and men are more likely to initiate or be receptive to sexual activity while intoxicated. Yet the more alcohol an individual consumes, the more likely he is to experience sexual problems, such as erectile dysfunction and either premature or delayed ejaculation. Alcohol is a depressant of the central nervous system, and healthy sexual functioning is related to a healthy nervous system. Long-term alcohol use is associated with lowered testosterone levels and decreased sexual desire. Alcohol use impairs an individual's ability to make healthy decisions about sexual activity. Alcohol has also been shown to increase aggression in some individuals, which can lead to violence and forcing others to engage in nonconsensual sexual activities.

Marijuana. Marijuana appears to have little direct effect on sexual functioning; however, chronic use has been linked to decreased sperm production. Men sometimes believe that marijuana will improve sex, but, in general, both men and women report decreased sexual desire when using the drug.

Cocaine. Many men believe that cocaine sexually excites women and that it improves men's ability to maintain erections. Low doses of cocaine do seem to increase testosterone levels; however, higher doses have the opposite effect. Cocaine activates the pleasure centers in the brain in ways that are very similar to the ways in which sex affects the brain. Thus, using cocaine can trigger a desire for sex, and engaging in sexual activity can stimulate a desire to use the drug. Chronic use of cocaine may lead to decreased sexual desire, erectile dysfunction, and delayed orgasm.

Methamphetamine. Methamphetamines do not seem to have a direct effect on sexual functioning in low doses. Higher doses and chronic use may lead to decreased libido and erectile dysfunction. The drug enhances a person's sense of general well-being and excitement, which may lower sexual inhibitions. Methamphetamine use is linked to high-risk sexual behaviors, including violence. Intravenous use increases the risk of exposure to HIV. Long-term methamphetamine use is physically debilitating and results in decreased sexual desire and functioning.

Heroin. Heroin and other opiate drugs (such as morphine, methadone, codeine, and oxycodone) lower the metabolic rate and tend to suppress sexual desire and functioning. Intravenous use increases the risk of exposure to HIV. Chronic heroin users consistently report an inability to maintain an erection and achieve orgasm.

Although alcohol and other drugs can increase sexual response initially, chronic use tends to deteriorate all areas of sexual response for both men and women. For an addict, the physical, emotional, and behavioral damage of chemical use inevitably has a negative effect on sexuality and sexual functioning.

Behavioral Effects

Alcohol and other drug use can have serious effects on sexual behavior. Following are some common problematic and harmful behaviors.

- Taking advantage of an inebriated or drugged partner
- Date rape
- Infidelity, having affairs
- Unprotected sex
- Sexual abuse
- Other risky sexual behaviors
- Compulsive sexual behavior
- Avoiding intimacy other than physical interaction
- Neglecting partner's needs and desires
- Avoiding physical relationships
- Dishonest or manipulative actions to have sex
- Going along with a peer group's behavior in violation of personal values
- Using chemicals to give oneself permission to act out sexually

When you were using, you may have engaged in sexual behavior that you feel ashamed of. You may have confused sexual desire with intimacy or love. Looking at and talking about these painful memories will help you begin the process of healing.

You may want to talk privately with your counselor or another professional person about some of these behaviors.

You may wish to make some notes here.

A Man's Workbook

The Sexual-Chemical Lifeline

The Sexual-Chemical Lifeline is a way to begin seeing the relationship between your use of alcohol or other drugs and your sexual behavior. A sample lifeline appears on the following page. On the page after that is a blank lifeline chart. On it you will chart your history of addiction and your sexual history, then look to see how they have affected each other. Draw your chemical history as a dotted line and your sexual history as a solid line.

On the sample lifeline, you can see that the straight horizontal line is the baseline. It is marked 5, 10, 15, and so on. Those numbers represent your age. On the left side of the chart is a vertical line labeled +10, 0, and –10. Events that are pleasant experiences fall in the 0 to +10 range, from okay to really great. Painful events fall in the 0 to –10 range. The more painful the event, the closer it is to –10.

As you look back at your past to identify your sexual experiences, you may remember events that you had previously forgotten or you may be surprised at how painful some of your memories are. You may become aware of certain patterns, especially patterns between chemical and sexual activities. It is not uncommon to find that, as your addiction progressed, your sexual experiences became less pleasant. By charting your Sexual-Chemical Lifeline, you can begin to become more aware of your sexual self when you were drinking or using. Then you can start thinking about your sexual self in recovery and consider what changes you would like to make.

Tom's Sexual-Chemical Lifeline

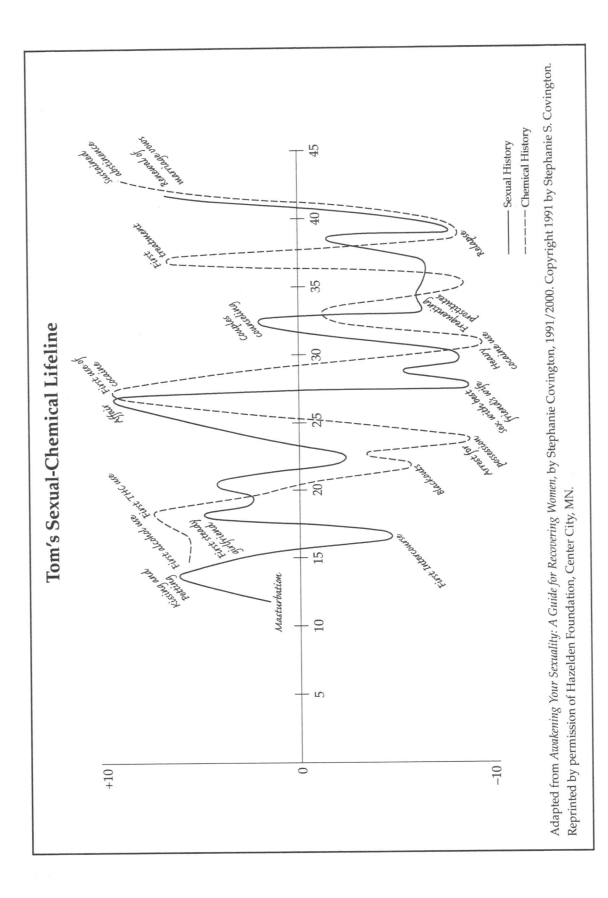

Sexual History
Chemical History

Masturbation
First Intercourse
Kissing and petting
First alcohol use
First THC use
First steady girlfriend
Affair
First use of cocaine
Blackouts
Arrest for possession
Sex with best friend's wife
Heavy cocaine use
Frequenting prostitutes
Couples counseling
First treatment
Relapse
Renewal of marriage vows
Sustained abstinence

Adapted from *Awakening Your Sexuality: A Guide for Recovering Women*, by Stephanie Covington, 1991/2000. Copyright 1991 by Stephanie S. Covington. Reprinted by permission of Hazelden Foundation, Center City, MN.

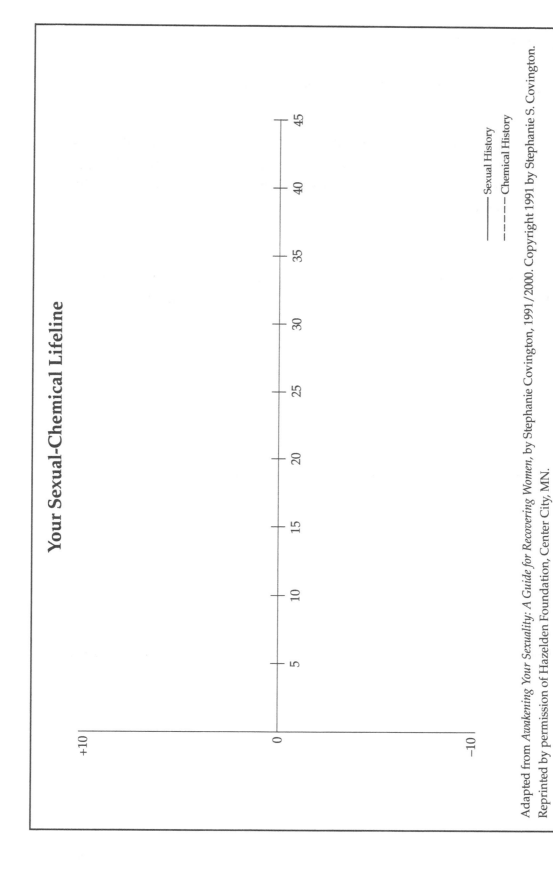

Your Sexual-Chemical Lifeline

+10

0

−10

5   10   15   20   25   30   35   40   45

——— Sexual History
− − − − Chemical History

Adapted from *Awakening Your Sexuality: A Guide for Recovering Women*, by Stephanie Covington, 1991/2000. Copyright 1991 by Stephanie S. Covington. Reprinted by permission of Hazelden Foundation, Center City, MN.

Assignment

The assignment to be completed before the next session follows:

Complete your Sexual-Chemical Lifeline. Then give some thought to the questions below. At the beginning of the next group session, you will have the opportunity to share your responses to these issues. You can make some notes in the spaces provided.

1. As your alcohol or other drug use increased, what effect did this have on your dating, your marriage, and/or your sexual behavior in general?

2. Describe any specific sexual behaviors or incidents that harmed you.

3. Describe any specific sexual behaviors or incidents that harmed another person.

A Man's Workbook

4. Describe any specific sexual behaviors or incidents that violated your value system.

5. Did you ever use alcohol or other drugs to enhance a sexual experience or to give yourself permission to engage in a particular sexual behavior? Explain.

6. Is there anything you are willing to share regarding your sexual history that causes you feelings of guilt, shame, anger, hurt, or confusion? Explain.

Reflections on Recovery

At first, it can be extremely difficult to talk about sex in an open and honest manner with other men. You may not be sure what to say and what not to say. You may have some very painful or confusing memories and feelings about your sexuality. You may be relieved that others have had some of the same experiences you have had. Maybe you are glad that you have finally found a place where you can be open about your questions. Whatever you're feeling is absolutely valid.

Use the space below to record any thoughts you have about the material covered in today's session.

Into Action

This is an optional activity. An example of an action step relating to this session is to have a conversation with your partner about sex. Talk about what you enjoy, what you don't enjoy, and what you would like to do differently. If you are currently in custody, here is a different example. You could have a conversation with one of the group members or other trusted friend about how you are managing your sexuality while incarcerated. What you choose to do does not necessarily have to relate to the material covered in this session; however, it should relate in some way to your recovery.

Use the space below to describe what action step you will take between now and the next session. You also can record what results were achieved.

Recovery Scale

Please take a few moments to mark the degree to which you do each of the following things. Make an "X" or a circle on each line to indicate your response. You will complete this form again at the end of this module on Sexuality to see how you have changed. You will not have to compare your answers with anyone else's, and you will not be judged on how well you are doing. This is not a test but an opportunity for you to chart your own progress in recovery. If you currently are in custody, some of the items may not be relevant now. You can cross them out or just not respond to them. (If you know your release date, you may want to think about how you would like your life to be in the future.)

	Not at All	Just a Little	Pretty Much	Very Much
1. I am comfortable with my body.				
2. I can talk to professionals, including my counselor and my doctor, about sexual concerns.				
3. I can speak appropriately with other men about sexual matters.				
4. I can be affectionate with others.				
5. I am comfortable with my sexual identity.				
6. I can accept sexual pleasure from my partner.				
7. I consider my partner's sexual needs and preferences.				
8. I can express my sexual desires to my partner.				
9. I am comfortable having sober sex.				
10. I believe that pleasing myself sexually is healthy.				
11. I understand that sexuality is about more than the physical act of sex.				

Sexual Identity

Sexual Characteristics

In our society, we tend to think of masculinity and femininity as rigid categories, and we think that men look a certain way, act in certain ways, and like certain things. However, most men have many characteristics that you might think of as being feminine. When you were young, you might have been discouraged from expressing any of these "feminine" traits. You may have been criticized or teased because of them. This may have led you to reject, deny, or be ashamed of those parts of yourself that don't neatly fit the definition of "manly." And you may have been led to believe that the traits associated with masculinity are valued more highly than the traits associated with femininity.

1. Use the space that follows to list any of your traits, characteristics, preferences, activities, and so on that might be considered feminine in nature.

2. How comfortable are you with these aspects of yourself?

3. Have there been times when you avoided doing or saying something that you wanted to do or say, just because you were afraid that it would be interpreted as unmanly? If so, give a specific example.

4. Have you ever criticized or teased another boy or man for exhibiting feminine characteristics? If so, give a specific example.

A Man's Workbook

5. If you have been taught to be critical of feminine characteristics, what effect has this had on the way that you think about girls and women?

Sexual Orientation

In our society, there are many negative and confusing messages about sexuality. For example, many people think that a person is either "straight" or "gay" and that this can be determined easily by whether the person has sex with men or women. Although you may believe that someone is completely gay or completely straight, and that a person is born one way and stays that way throughout life, research indicates that, for some people, sexual identity is neither absolute nor fixed. Sexual identity can be fluid and exists across a continuum from exclusively homosexual to bisexual to exclusively heterosexual.

Since early childhood, you probably have been exposed to a wide variety of opinions about gay men; unfortunately, many of them were probably negative. If you are homosexual, these messages may have caused you to hide your sexual preferences from others or to feel ashamed of who you are. If you are heterosexual, these messages may have caused you to feel compelled to prove to others (and perhaps to yourself) that you are straight. Both straight and gay men are affected by homophobia, which is defined as "an irrational fear of, aversion to, or discrimination against homosexuality or homosexuals."

In one of the earlier sessions, you identified the rules of being a man. If you think about these rules again, you will see that many of them are about not being "feminine" and not being "gay." Boys and men who break these rules are criticized, mocked, humiliated, and even physically abused. This is one of the primary reasons that many men struggle with fully accepting every aspect of who they are. And it is one of the primary reasons that many men have so much trouble developing intimate relationships with other men.

1. What feelings have you had as the result of this session?

2. How safe and comfortable do you feel talking about sexual orientation and sexual identity?

3. What issues did this session raise that you would like to discuss with your counselor or another professional?

The Sex Funnel

In a previous session, you learned about the anger funnel and how men tend to turn painful feelings like hurt, fear, and shame into anger. There also is a sex funnel, in which we channel all our feelings of closeness and affection, for people of both sexes, and they come out as sexual desire. As a result, for some men, having sex is the only way they know to be intimate. This may cause men so much shame that it leads to some really inappropriate and even dangerous behavior. It may also cause men to become confused about their feelings toward women and other men.

The sex funnel is a good symbol to represent the sexualization of emotions. This is just a fancy way of saying that if you experience strong feelings of affection in a relationship, it is very easy to make it all about sex. This may prevent you from having intimate friendships with other men and may lead to excessive reliance on women to satisfy your emotional needs. The sex funnel also inhibits men's ability to have non-sexual, yet intimate, relationships with women.

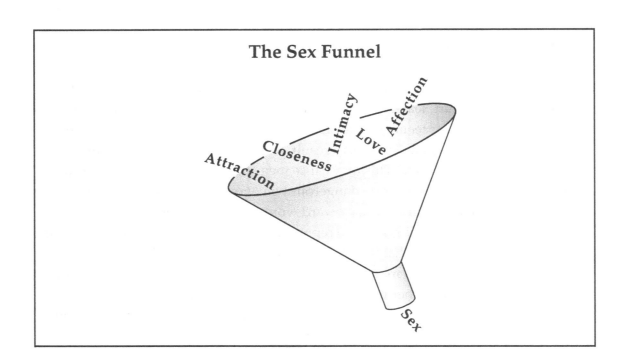

The Sex Funnel

A Man's Workbook

Answer the following two questions in the spaces provided.

1. How do you see the sex funnel operating in your life?

2. If you were to change the way that the sex funnel works in your life, how might your relationships change?

Assignment

The assignment to be completed before the next session follows:

Complete the Sexual Attitudes and Behavior Scale that follows. You will not have to share any of the details from this assignment with your fellow group members.

Sexual Attitudes and Behavior Scale

Circle the number on the scale that indicates where you see yourself now; draw an arrow to where you would like to be. If you are living in a residential treatment setting or correctional facility, some of the items may not be relevant to your life now, but you can still indicate where you would like to be in the future.

I am unable to communicate verbally with my partner about my sexual likes and dislikes.   I am able to communicate verbally with my partner about my sexual likes and dislikes.

| 1 | 2 | 3 | 4 | 5 | 6 | 7 | 8 | 9 | 10 |

I don't know what excites and turns me on sexually.   I know what turns me on sexually.

| 1 | 2 | 3 | 4 | 5 | 6 | 7 | 8 | 9 | 10 |

I am uncomfortable touching or looking at my naked body.   I am very comfortable touching or looking at my naked body.

| 1 | 2 | 3 | 4 | 5 | 6 | 7 | 8 | 9 | 10 |

I think that masturbation is a sin, is wrong, or I feel guilty about doing it.   I think that masturbation is healthy and a way to care for myself.

| 1 | 2 | 3 | 4 | 5 | 6 | 7 | 8 | 9 | 10 |

I get few of my sexual needs taken care of.   I get most of my sexual needs taken care of.

| 1 | 2 | 3 | 4 | 5 | 6 | 7 | 8 | 9 | 10 |

I think that my body is not very attractive.   I think that my body is very attractive.

| 1 | 2 | 3 | 4 | 5 | 6 | 7 | 8 | 9 | 10 |

I must be in love to really enjoy sex.   I can enjoy sex if I decide to; I don't have to be in love.

| 1 | 2 | 3 | 4 | 5 | 6 | 7 | 8 | 9 | 10 |

I usually make sure that taking care of my sexual needs is the priority.								I find that I want to receive and give pleasure equally.	
1	2	3	4	5	6	7	8	9	10

My sexual activity tends to always be the same.								I like to engage in a wide variety of sexual activities.	
1	2	3	4	5	6	7	8	9	10

I never care whether my partner is wanting to have sex.								I always make sure that sexual activities are consensual and mutually desired.	
1	2	3	4	5	6	7	8	9	10

I always worry about whether my sexual performance is good enough.								I never worry much about my sexual performance.	
1	2	3	4	5	6	7	8	9	10

I use pornography and masturbate more than I'm comfortable with.								I am comfortable with the way that I give myself pleasure.	
1	2	3	4	5	6	7	8	9	10

Adapted from *Working with Women's Groups* (Vol. 2), by Louise Yolton Eberhardt, 1994. Duluth, MN: Whole Person Associates, Inc. Copyright 1994 by Louise Yolton Eberhardt. Reprinted with permission.

Reflections on Recovery

This may have been a difficult session for you. You probably have not had much previous opportunity to explore some of these issues. You may have been raised to have strong feelings about sexuality and sexual practices. You may even have been told that it isn't proper to have these kinds of discussions.

Beliefs about sexuality can be influenced by age, religious tradition, cultural background, and socioeconomic class. The goal of these discussions is not to convert you to a particular way of thinking but to provide you with an opportunity to consider new information and ideas and to help you to establish your own comfort zone with your sexuality.

Use the space below to record any thoughts you have about the material covered in today's session.

Into Action

This is an optional activity. What you choose to do does not necessarily have to relate to the material covered in this session; however, it should relate in some way to your recovery.

Use the space below to describe what action step you will take between now and the next session. You also can record what results were achieved.

Barriers to Sexual Health

Sexual Abuse

In Session 7, we discussed sexual abuse within the context of unhealthy relationships. This issue is so critical to the process of recovery for a significant percentage of men that we will be revisiting it in this session. We know two things about men and sexual abuse: (1) most men do not admit to childhood sexual abuse until they are adults, if ever, and (2) the incidence of sexual abuse among boys and men is considerably underreported. Historically, there has been a taboo in our society against speaking about men as victims of sexual abuse. Therefore, until recently, it was not considered a critical issue for men.

Alcohol and other drugs cloud the memory, so when a man becomes sober, painful memories can begin to surface. A recovering man might decide that it's finally time to deal with his sexual past. If you have been sexually abused, it was wrong and it was not your fault. It does not indicate anything about who you are as a man. Although abusive experiences can affect your overall sexual health, the abuse does not define your sexuality. Discussing sexual abuse with a counselor can help you begin the process of healing.

If you have been sexually abusive to another person in the past, it was wrong. If you are currently being sexually abusive to another person, it is wrong, and it needs to stop right now. Sexual activity between an adult and a child or an adolescent, regardless of either's gender, constitutes abuse.

167

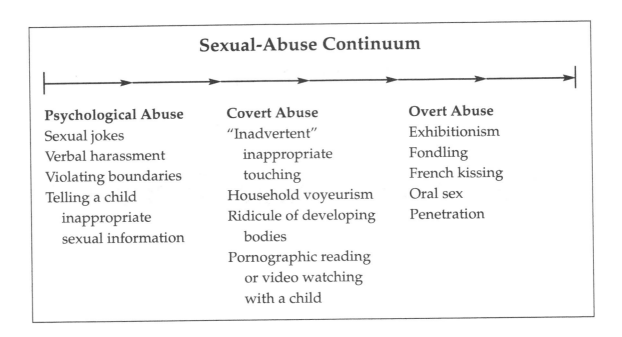

Sexual-Abuse Continuum

Psychological Abuse
Sexual jokes
Verbal harassment
Violating boundaries
Telling a child
    inappropriate
    sexual information

Covert Abuse
"Inadvertent"
    inappropriate
    touching
Household voyeurism
Ridicule of developing
    bodies
Pornographic reading
    or video watching
    with a child

Overt Abuse
Exhibitionism
Fondling
French kissing
Oral sex
Penetration

Are there any issues relating to sex abuse that you should talk to a counselor about? If so, you can make notes about them here.

Nonconsensual Sex

A widely held belief about sexual relationships is that "anything is okay as long as it's between two or more consenting adults and does not create harm." It is important in recovery to examine what you believe the word "consenting" means. You can easily identify some sexual activities that are clearly nonconsensual, such as rape. But there are other sexual acts that you may not have thought of as being nonconsensual. For example: what if a man goes out on a date with a woman and buys her drinks even after it's obvious that she is becoming impaired? He does this because he believes that she is more likely to go along with having sex if she is drunk. If they do have inter-

A Man's Workbook

course, is this consensual? Is it consensual if a man threatens to withhold financial support unless his partner agrees to meet his sexual demands?

1. In the space below, list some other examples of nonconsensual sex.

2. When your addiction was active, did you ever engage in nonconsensual sex? If so, give a specific example.

3. What are some steps that you can take as a recovering and sexually healthy man to ensure that you don't engage in nonconsensual sex?

Masturbation and Sex Addiction

A sexual behavior that can be quite confusing for men is masturbation. It is rarely discussed and almost universally practiced. From the onset of puberty throughout adulthood and into old age, men masturbate. Even men who are in sexually fulfilling relationships masturbate. Men masturbate for a variety of reasons: to relieve stress, to help themselves fall asleep, to experience pleasure, and to explore their own sexuality. Masturbation for any of these reasons is not harmful or unhealthy. What is harmful and unhealthy is the guilt, shame, and confusion that some men feel about masturbation when their behavior is perfectly normal.

However, even something healthy can become problematic if it gets out of balance. Some men who have experienced problems with alcohol or other drugs might have had a concurrent sexual addiction or compulsion. Other men might develop a sexual addiction after becoming sober. Sexual addiction is characterized by repetitive and intense sexual fantasies, sexual urges, and/or sexual behaviors that cause negative consequences to your physical and/or emotional well-being, relationships, job, and other important life areas.

The following behaviors are warning signs of sexual addiction. Doing or experiencing any of these things does not mean that you are a sex addict. However, if you are experiencing any of these warning signs, you should talk to your counselor or another professional for evaluation.

- Masturbating excessively, at inappropriate times, and/or in inappropriate places
- Needing more and more extreme forms of pornography to become sexually aroused when masturbating
- Frequently using sex services, such as telephone lines, strip clubs, massage parlors, and prostitutes
- Compulsively looking for sexual partners
- Having constant sexual activity be the most important aspect of your relationship with your partner
- Using sexual activity to deal with uncomfortable feelings
- Being secretive or dishonest about your sexual activities
- Continually seeking more and more intense sexual experiences
- Frequently moving from relationship to relationship, seeking new sexual partners and experiences
- Finding it emotionally unbearable to do without sex for brief periods of time

- Having sexual preoccupation or behavior result in your avoiding or ignoring all other forms of intimate connection
- Participating in high-risk sexual behaviors despite adverse consequences

Sexual Triggers

The first months and even years of recovery can be quite challenging. A lot of negative feelings may come to the surface. Many of these feelings would have led you to using in the past. Now you have made the decision to no longer use alcohol or other drugs as a coping mechanism. Consequently, it is not unusual to find yourself turning to some form of sex to help you deal with your feelings. The problem is that you may be in danger of substituting one set of addictive or harmful behaviors for another. And engaging in even healthy sexual activity may be a relapse trigger for you.

Addiction causes chemical changes in the brain. Your brain became accustomed to the pleasurable feelings generated by alcohol or other drugs. Now that the chemicals are gone, your brain still wants to feel a certain way. Sex can help to provide those pleasurable feelings or take uncomfortable feelings away, because the chemical release that accompanies sex might remind your brain of using. Therefore, sexual activity in early recovery could trigger the desire to use chemicals. Another risk is that you may not find sexual activities as intense as they were when you were using, so you might feel a desire to get drunk or high in order to recapture that physical sensation. Finally, you may not have much experience with initiating or consummating sexual activity when you are sober. The fear of rejection, loneliness, or inadequate performance might make you crave a chemical boost.

Answer the following questions in the spaces provided.

1. Are there any attitudes or sexual behaviors from your past that might pose a threat to your recovery? Explain. (For example: "I used to go to topless clubs with my friends. If I were to do that now, it would definitely cause a craving to drink.")

2. Are there any attitudes or sexual behaviors occurring currently that could pose a threat to your recovery? Explain. (For example: "Right now I am not comfortable dating and I'm avoiding all possible sexual opportunities. If this continues for a long time, I am going to become really lonely and frustrated.")

3. Are there any attitudes or sexual behaviors that might occur in the future that could potentially pose a threat to your recovery? Explain. (For example: "I used drugs practically every time I had sex and I relied on them to aid my performance. If I find that I can't perform or enjoy sex as much without drugs, I might be tempted to use again.")

A Man's Workbook

Assignment

The assignment to be completed before the next session follows:

In the space below, write your three greatest fears about your sexuality as a recovering man. Then share these with another man (a male family member, a friend, an A.A. or N.A. acquaintance, or a fellow group member). Record what this experience was like for you.

Reflections on Recovery

Most men in early recovery are concerned about what it will be like to be sexual without the aid of alcohol or other drugs. Will it be any good? Will I be able to last as long as I did when I was high? Where will I meet sexual partners? If you have been having such concerns, you are not alone. Any feelings of insecurity that you may have about sex become more apparent to you when you are sober and chemicals are not masking your fears. You may begin to think you are doomed to having no sex, not enough sex, or unsatisfying sex for the rest of your life. Talking about these fears and concerns with other recovering men will go a long way toward helping you feel more comfortable and confident. It also will help you begin to create a new, healthy, and satisfying sexual life for yourself.

Use the space that follows to record any thoughts you have about the material covered in today's session.

Into Action

This is an optional activity. What you choose to do does not necessarily have to relate to the material covered in this session; however, it should relate in some way to your recovery.

Use the space below to describe what action step you will take between now and the next session. You also can record what results were achieved.

Healthy Sexuality

Body Image

Our society places a great deal of emphasis on physical appearance. Both men and women are led to believe that their value as human beings is directly related to their appearance. You are bombarded daily with images and messages saying that you must be tall, muscular, fit, have a flat stomach, and have a full head of hair in order to be sexually successful and to advance in a career. Products are sold on television and in magazines that will reverse baldness, increase muscle tone, eliminate wrinkles, and increase the size of your penis.

Your body is an essential part of who you are. If you are uncomfortable with or hate your body, you hate part of yourself. It is important for a recovering man to learn to love, respect, and accept his body.

On the following pages are two outlines of a man's body. The first represents the front of your body, and the second represents the back of your body. Fill in these figures by marking them in one of three ways:

- Mark the parts of your body that you like and feel satisfied with by using plus signs, like this:

    + + + + +

- Mark the parts you do not like, hate, or feel uncomfortable with by using minus signs, like this:

    − − − − −

175

- Mark the parts of your body that you feel neutral about by using little circles, like this:

  ○ ○ ○ ○ ○

You will not be asked to share this work with anyone else. It is intended to help you to become more aware of how you regard your body.

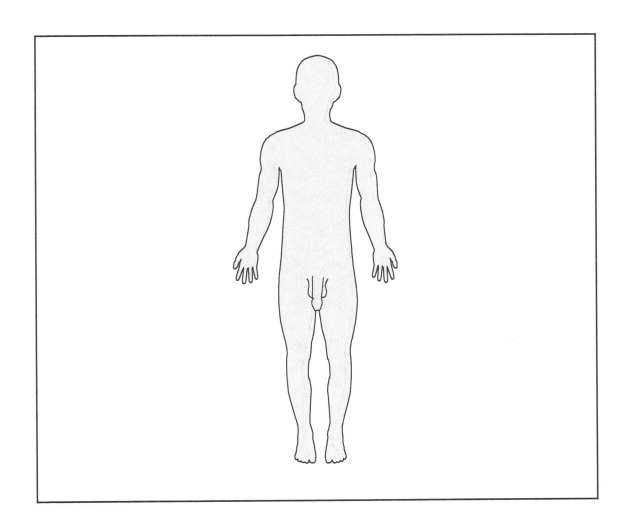

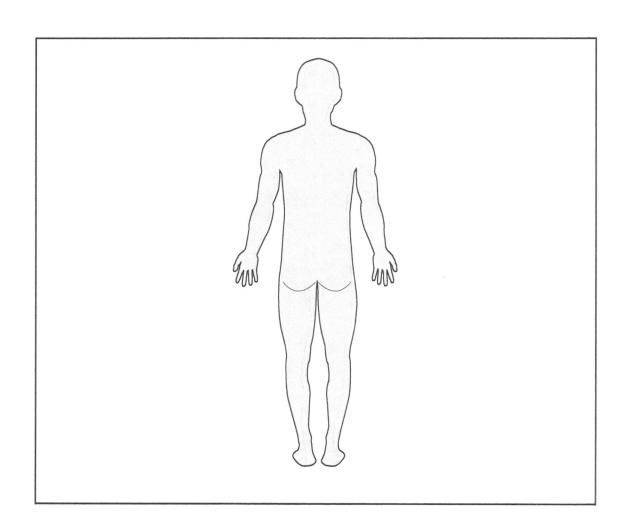

Think about the body parts that you dislike or feel uncomfortable with. Some of these, such as your height, can't be changed. You may want to work on being more accepting of these physical features. Some of these, such as your weight, can be altered through diet, exercise, or other means. You may decide that you would like to improve these features. Use the space below to record your thoughts after completing this exercise.

Sexual Health

You have spent several sessions exploring the issue of male sexuality and the ways in which your sexuality is a critical component of your recovery process. Perhaps this is the first time that you have fully explored your sexuality and have talked with other men about your experiences, your thoughts, and your feelings. You may now have a sense of what types of behaviors are problematic or unhealthy but still have some confusion about exactly what constitutes healthy sexuality. The following diagram represents a model of sexual health.

Sexual Health Model

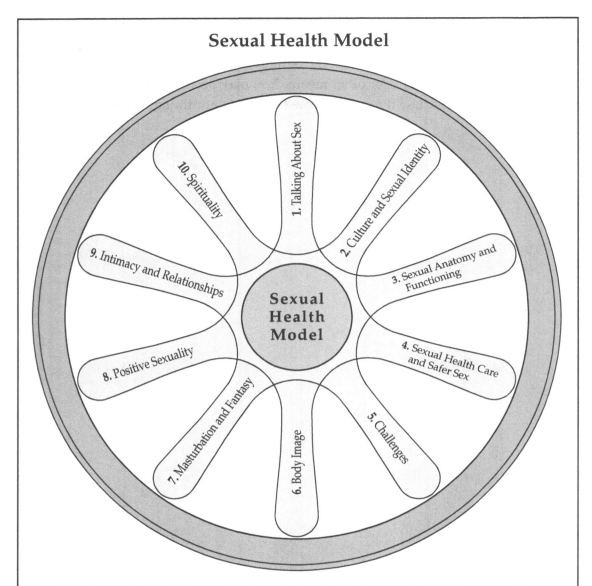

From "The Sexual Health Model: Application of a Sexological Approach to HIV Prevention," by B. Robinson, W. O. Bockting, S. Rosser, D. L. Rugg, M. Miner, and E. Coleman, 2002. *Health Education Research: Theory and Practice, 17*(1), pp. 43–57. Copyright 2002 by Oxford University Press. Adapted with permission.

A Man's Workbook

Each spoke of the wheel represents a principle of healthy sexuality. How you choose to apply these principles in your life is a matter of personal choice. The principles are as follows:

1. **Talking About Sex**. A key part of the Sexual Health Model is the ability to talk comfortably and explicitly about sexuality, especially one's own sexual values, preferences, attractions, history, and behaviors. Being able to talk about sex is necessary and is a valuable skill that must be learned and practiced. There is a simple saying: "If you can't talk about sex, you should not be having it."

2. **Culture and Sexual Identity**. Culture influences one's sexuality and sense of sexual self. It is important that individuals examine their culture as it relates to their sexual identities, attitudes, behaviors, and health.

3. **Sexual Anatomy and Functioning**. Sexual health assumes a basic knowledge, understanding, and acceptance of one's sexual anatomy, sexual response, and sexual functioning. Sexual health includes freedom from sexual dysfunction and other sexual problems.

4. **Sexual Health Care and Safer Sex**. Sexual health covers knowing one's body, performing regular self-exams for cancer and STDs, and responding to physical changes with appropriate medical intervention. Take care of your body, and your body will take care of you.

5. **Challenges: Overcoming Barriers to Sexual Health**. Challenges to sexual health are all the things the group talked about in the last session: sexual abuse, addiction, compulsive sexual behavior, sex work, harassment, and discrimination. Because men are pushed toward unhealthy sexual attitudes and behaviors, we have to confront them directly as we explore our sexual health.

6. **Body Image**. In a culture obsessed with a type of physical beauty that few of us will ever achieve, a realistic, positive body image is an important aspect of sexual health. This can be difficult to achieve. Challenging the notion of one narrow standard of attractiveness and encouraging self-acceptance is relevant to all populations.

7. **Masturbation and Fantasy**. In our culture, the topics of masturbation and fantasy are surrounded by misunderstanding and confusion, because most of us do not grow up exposed to healthy conversations about these subjects. However, they can be part of healthy sexuality when they are in balance with the rest of the spokes of the Sexual Health Model. Fantasies about children or about nonconsensual sex are not healthy.

8. **Positive Sexuality**. All human beings need to explore their sexuality in order to develop and nurture who they are. Exploring and celebrating sexuality from a positive and self-affirming perspective is an essential feature of sexual health. Positive sexuality includes appropriate experimentation, affirming sensuality, attaining sexual competence through the ability to give and receive sexual pleasure, and setting sexual boundaries based on what one prefers as well as what one knows is safe and responsible.

9. **Intimacy and Relationships**. Intimacy is a universal need that people try to meet through their relationships. There are different kinds of intimacy. Knowing which intimacy needs are important for you is helpful in getting these needs met.

10. **Spirituality**. Our definition of sexual health assumes that a person's ethical, spiritual, and moral beliefs and his sexual behaviors and values are aligned. In this context, spirituality may not include religion but it needs to address moral and ethical concerns and deeper values. This helps us to integrate our sexual and spiritual selves. Your group will talk a lot about this in the final three sessions.

A Man's Workbook

Making a Collage

This activity provides you an opportunity to examine your ideas about healthy sexuality in a creative way. Creating a collage that represents your vision of your ideal sexual self is a form of self-expression. Sometimes it is not easy to verbalize what you feel good about, and many people find that it is easier to get in touch with deep and meaningful truths through dance or song or poetry or art. Like other art, the technique of collage uses visual imagery to express what may not be easy for you to express in words.

To make your collage, you will use magazines and cut or tear out pictures and words that represent your vision of sexual health. If you see a picture in a magazine that "speaks" to you, use it. Try not to think too much about it. The pictures you use and your collage do not even have to "make sense." Trust your creative instincts. You also can use pens or colored markers to write words, phrases, or symbols. Use a glue stick to arrange your pictures and words on your cardboard or poster board.

You may be skeptical or feel uncomfortable about participating in this activity. Remember that one of the main themes of this program is that recovery is a process of growth and expansion. Another main theme is about letting go of some of the old rules about what men do and don't do. Allow yourself to play, have fun, be creative, and see what happens.

After completing your collage, answer the following two questions in the spaces provided.

1. What was it like for you to make a collage about healthy sexuality?

2. How do the images and words you selected represent your vision of sexual health?

A Man's Workbook

Sexual Rights

Sexual rights are universal human rights based on the inherent freedom, dignity, and equality of all human beings. Because health is a fundamental human right, so should sexual health be a basic human right. If you currently are living in a residential treatment or correctional facility, you may not have all the rights listed below.

World Association of Sexual Health (WAS) Declaration of Sexual Rights

1. **The right to sexual freedom**. Sexual freedom encompasses the possibility for individuals to express their full sexual potential. However, this excludes all forms of sexual coercion, exploitation, and abuse at any time and in any situations in life.

2. **The right to sexual autonomy, sexual integrity, and safety of the sexual body**. This right involves the ability to make autonomous decisions about one's sexual life within a context of one's own personal and social ethics. It also encompasses control and enjoyment of our own bodies free from torture, mutilation, and violence of any sort.

3. **The right to sexual privacy**. This involves the right for individual decisions and behaviors about intimacy as long as they do not intrude on the sexual rights of others.

4. **The right to sexual equality**. This refers to freedom from all forms of discrimination, regardless of sex, gender, sexual orientation, age, race, social class, religion, or physical and emotional disability.

5. **The right to sexual pleasure**. Sexual pleasure, including autoeroticism, is a source of physical, psychological, intellectual, and spiritual well-being.

6. **The right to emotional sexual expression**. Sexual expression is more than erotic pleasure or sexual acts. Individuals have a right to express their sexuality through communication, touch, emotional expression, and love.

7. **The right to sexually associate freely**. This means the possibility to marry or not, to divorce, and to establish other types of responsible sexual associations.

(Continued)

World Association of Sexual Health (WAS) Declaration of Sexual Rights (Continued)

8. **The right to make free and responsible reproductive choices**. This encompasses the right to decide whether or not to have children, the number and spacing of children, and the right to full access to the means of fertility regulation.

9. **The right to sexual information based upon scientific inquiry**. This right implies that sexual information should be generated through the process of unencumbered, yet scientifically ethical, inquiry and disseminated in appropriate ways at all societal levels.

10. **The right to comprehensive sexuality education**. This is a lifelong process from birth throughout the life cycle and should involve all social institutions.

11. **The right to sexual health care**. Sexual health care should be available for prevention and treatment of all sexual concerns, problems, and disorders.

The Declaration of Sexual Rights was adopted at the 14th World Congress of Sexology, August 26, 1999, Hong Kong. Reprinted with permission of World Association of Sexual Health (www .worldsexology.org).

A Man's Workbook

Assignment

The assignment to be completed before the next session follows:

Use the space provided to write a paragraph describing how you want your sexuality to be in the future. Imagine that it is one year from now (or one year after your release). What does your sexual life look like? Who else is involved? How do you feel? Try to incorporate what you have learned about problematic behaviors, shameful feelings, healthy sexuality, and sexual rights.

Reflections on Recovery

Thus far, you have explored the concepts of healthy relationships and healthy sexuality. But you have not been asked to look specifically at the concept of "love." Love is perhaps the most gratifying and most complicated of human emotions. Men look for and need love more than they may be willing to admit.

You may think of love as a feeling, but, more important, love is also a behavior. Feeling love is easy, but being a loving person is much more difficult. Three things are necessary for love: respect, mutuality, and compassion.

> **Respect** is the appreciation of someone's values, and it begins when we perceive the person's integrity. We often earn respect when we are willing to do the right thing, particularly when the choice is difficult.
>
> **Mutuality** means there is an equal investment in the relationship. Each person has a willingness and desire to "see" the other as well as to be seen; to hear the other as well as to be heard; and to be vulnerable as well as to respect the other's vulnerability. Mutuality also means that there is an awareness of the "we," not merely of the two individuals.
>
> **Compassion** is similar to empathy but it occurs on a deeper level. Empathy is understanding another's feelings and being able to feel along with the person. Compassion is caring deeply about another person's struggle or pain and wanting to help alleviate it. When we are compassionate, we lend ourselves to another's process; we give of ourselves in order to be with the other person emotionally.

The quotation is from *Beyond Trauma: A Healing Journey for Women*, by Stephanie Covington, 2003, p. 189. Copyright 2003 by Stephanie S. Covington. Reprinted by permission of Hazelden Foundation, Center City, MN.

Use the space below to record any thoughts you have about the material covered in today's session.

Into Action

This is an optional activity. What you choose to do does not necessarily have to relate to the material covered in this session; however, it should relate in some way to your recovery.

Use the space below to describe what action step you will take between now and the next session. You also can record what results were achieved.

Recovery Scale

Please take a few moments to mark the degree to which you do each of the following things. You assessed yourself on this scale at the beginning of this module. Please reassess yourself to see where you are now. You will not have to compare your answers with anyone else, nor will you be judged on how well you do. This is not a test but an opportunity for you to chart your progress in recovery. Skip or cross out the items that are not relevant at this time. After you finish this scale, go back and look at the one you did earlier.

	Not at All	Just a Little	Pretty Much	Very Much
1. I am comfortable with my body.				
2. I can talk to professionals, including my counselor and my doctor, about sexual concerns.				
3. I can speak appropriately with other men about sexual matters.				
4. I can be affectionate with others.				
5. I am comfortable with my sexual identity.				
6. I can accept sexual pleasure from my partner.				
7. I consider my partner's sexual needs and preferences.				
8. I can express my sexual desires to my partner.				
9. I am comfortable having sober sex.				
10. I believe that pleasing myself sexually is healthy.				
11. I understand that sexuality is about more than the physical act of sex.				

190

MODULE D

Spirituality

What Is Spirituality?

Feeling Okay

Here is a new exercise, called "Five Senses," that you can use to help manage uncomfortable feelings, such as anxiety, fear, and stress. By focusing on your senses in the "here and now," you will be able to detach from any inner distress you may be experiencing.

1. Close your eyes and relax for about thirty seconds.
2. Open your eyes.
3. Silently, identify five things you can see around you.
4. Identify four things you can feel or touch.
5. Identify three things you can hear.
6. Now identify two things you can smell.
7. Finally, identify what you can taste right now.

As with all the grounding techniques you have learned, the more you practice the Five Senses exercise, the more effective it becomes. You can use all the exercises in this workbook in almost any environment when you are feeling stressed or uncomfortable.

Religion and Spirituality

It is believed that all humans have an inborn desire for spirituality, for wholeness and connection, or a relationship with a divine force. You may have a spiritual void inside that you are longing to have filled. You may desire something more than just achievements, possessions, approval, or pleasurable experiences. True spirituality is a connection with a force, power, or strength that is greater than you are. You move from living in a self-centered universe to living in a broad and ever-expanding universe in which you are only a small, but essential, part.

For some men, discomfort with the concept of spirituality is really discomfort with religion as they have observed or experienced it. Some of us have had positive experiences with religion, and others have not. Each man needs to find a relationship with something meaningful outside himself that works for him, and this will evolve over time. As you grow in recovery, your sense of spirituality likely will grow as well.

Answer the following five questions in the spaces provided:

1. Think back to your childhood. What was the role of religion in your family?

2. Was religion a positive experience for you then or a negative one? In what way?

3. Have you engaged in any nonreligious spiritual practices either as a child or as an adult? What have these been like for you?

4. What words come to mind when you think of spirituality?

5. Do you have any specific ideas or plans to bring more spirituality into your life now that you are sober? What are some of these?

Men of Service

Recovering men have discovered that one of the greatest tools to help them fill the spiritual void is being of service to others. Many have said that you experience true spirituality through your relationships with other people and your community. Being of service means helping other people, organizations, and social causes. It means giving of yourself in a way that makes your life, and the lives of others around you, better in some way. For example, active participation in A.A. or another Twelve Step group is a form of service (being there for another addict and sharing your experience, strength, and hope).

Think of a time in your life when you did something generous and selfless for another person, without any expectation of financial reward or approval. Remember what that felt like.

In the spaces below, write any ideas that you have about being of service to others. What are some things you would be willing to do that would deepen your connection to others in your community?

In the spaces below, write any ideas that you have about being of service to others. What are some things you would be willing to do that would deepen your connection to others in your community? If you currently are in jail or prison, remember that this is a community as well. You can be of service to others regardless of your environment or circumstances.

1.

2.

3.

4.

5.

6.

Being part of a community means not only giving of yourself to others but also allowing others to give to you. One of the greatest gifts that you can offer other people is the invitation to become part of your life. Men are raised to believe that they must be independent and self-sufficient, that asking another person for support or help is a sign of weakness. But you have learned that asking for and accepting support is a critical component in your struggle to overcome addiction. It also is an essential aspect of spiritual growth and healing.

In the space below, identify something in your life that you have been trying to do without help from anyone else and that you are tired of doing alone. An example is: "I have been trying to be a single father without any help from anyone else and I am tired of doing it alone."

I have been

and I am tired of doing it alone.

Assignment

The assignment to be completed before the next session follows:

Do something of service for another person or your community without expectation of financial reward. This could be as simple as volunteering a few hours of time at a local charitable organization or arriving early to an A.A. meeting to make the coffee and arrange the chairs. If you are in custody, ask the chaplain about volunteering some time to help another. In the space that follows, describe your act of service and how you felt afterward.

Reflections on Recovery

As a group participant in the *Helping Men Recover* program, you are already a member of a spiritual community and you have already begun your spiritual journey. Each time you have shared your thoughts and feelings or have been supportive to another group member, you have grown spiritually. The connections that you have made with your fellow participants are part of the spiritual foundation of your new life as a recovering man.

Use the space below to record any thoughts you have about the material covered in today's session.

Into Action

This is an optional activity. What you choose to do does not necessarily have to relate to the material covered in this session; however, it should relate in some way to your recovery. Some examples are

1. Ask a man at your Twelve Step meeting to be your sponsor.
2. If you are currently in custody, ask the chaplain or a social worker if there are any in-house opportunities to do volunteer or service work.
3. Mail a small, anonymous donation to your community's domestic violence shelter.

Use the space below to describe what action step you will take between now and the next session. You also can record what results were achieved.

Recovery Scale

Please take a few moments to mark the degree to which you do each of the things listed below. You can make an "X" or a circle on each line as your response. You will complete this form again at the end of this module on Spirituality to see how you have changed. You will not have to compare your answers with anyone else, nor will you be judged on how well you are doing. This is not a test but an opportunity for you to chart your own progress in recovery.

	Not at All	Just a Little	Pretty Much	Very Much
1. I acknowledge my spiritual needs.				
2. I understand the difference between religion and spirituality.				
3. I find comfort in my spiritual practices.				
4. I have a deep relationship and connection with a higher power.				
5. I feel connected to others.				
6. I respect the spiritual beliefs and practices of others.				
7. I practice some form of daily prayer or meditation.				
8. I am aware of my feelings of grief and loss.				
9. I trust my inner wisdom.				
10. I have a vision for my life.				
11. I live one day at a time.				
12. I am grateful for the life I have today.				

Real Men

Power and Privilege

In most Western cultures, men are a privileged group. Many men grow up believing that they should receive preferential treatment just because they are men. They hear this from other men and from women who were raised to believe the same thing. Both men and women have been constricted by the traditional roles imposed on them by society. Women are limited in what they are allowed to do, what they believe about themselves, and what they can aspire to. Men are limited in how they relate to others, what they are allowed to experience emotionally, and where they are supposed to dedicate their energies. Male-female relationships are inherently problematic as the result of this difference in power.

Answer the following questions in the spaces provided.

1. What are some of the rights or expectations that men grow up with?

2. What are the costs to women when you expect or demand these rights?

3. What are the costs to you when you expect or demand these rights?

4. How does this sense of entitlement affect the way in which you relate to other men?

The most common arena in which power and control are contested is the intimate relationship between a man and a woman. Heterosexual men are most likely to assume a privileged role with a spouse, partner, or girlfriend. The following are beliefs that some men have about male-female relationships.

A Man's Workbook

The Rights of Male Entitlement

1. To control her behavior
2. To make all decisions
3. To be in charge
4. To treat her like a servant
5. To treat her as your property
6. To be taken care of at home and at work (meals prepared, laundry done, coffee made)
7. To believe that, because you are a man, you are better than she is

Answer the following questions in the spaces provided.

1. Have you ever assumed that you had any of these rights?

2. How do you think the other people involved felt as a result of your behavior?

3. How did you feel after acting this way?

4. How do you feel about that behavior now?

Grief

When you first begin a recovery program, you may experience deep regret for how you have lived your life, and you may begin to grieve for the losses you have experienced as a result of addiction. You may be grieving your loss of freedom. You may begin to get in touch with feelings of grief for people and relationships that you have lost, including loved ones who have passed away. Perhaps you numbed these feelings with alcohol and other drugs or you simply avoided thinking about them, but now they are coming to the surface. Initially it may seem as though the feelings of grief will overwhelm you. You may be afraid that, if you acknowledge the grief, you will never stop hurting.

Merle Fossum wrote one of the first books about men and recovery; in it, he said this about grief:

> First we learn to surrender; then we feel the grief that follows; and then we must go back even further and surrender to the grief itself rather than beat it back. This is the process of transformation. This is how we work

with the mystery of powerlessness and allow change and growth into our lives. Through this mystery, a new healing occurs, and a feeling of peace, self-acceptance, and excitement comes over us.

Answer the following questions in the space provided.

1. On a scale of one to ten, with one representing no significant losses, what number would you assign to reflect the losses you have experienced in your life? Explain.

2. How did you deal with the most recent loss you experienced?

3. What are some of the fears that you have about dealing with grief and loss?

The quotation is from *Catching Fire: Men's Renewal and Recovery Through Crisis*, by Merle Fossum 1989, pp. 34–35. Center City, MN: Hazelden. Copyright 1989 by Hazelden Foundation. Reprinted with permission of Merle Fossum.

4. What would you need to feel safe enough to fully express your feelings of grief?

5. Do you have any unresolved grief issues? How important do these seem to you at this time?

A New Definition of Masculinity

In Session 2, you identified many of the rules for being a man that you learned from your family, at school, through the media, and so on. While some of these rules may have worked well for you, many of them are not consistent with how you want to lead your life in recovery. Now that you are clean and sober and have had the opportunity to explore some new ideas about masculinity, you are in a position to create some new rules for yourself.

1. What are the new rules you would like to live by with respect to how you deal with your feelings and other aspects of your inner life? An example is "My emotions are normal and natural, and it is healthy to share my feelings with other people in my life."

2. What are the new rules you would like to live by with respect to the important relationships in your life? An example is "Asking for help and support is a sign of strength and confidence, not an indication of weakness."

3. What are the new rules you would like to live by with respect to your sexuality? An example is "It's okay to express my sexuality in any way I want as long as I am not harming myself or another person."

4. What are the new rules you would like to live by with respect to your spirituality? An example is "I will give to others because it enriches me in the long run."

Meditation

Twelve Step programs such as A.A. encourage you to establish "conscious contact" with a higher power. Prayer and meditation are useful ways of developing and nurturing your spiritual self. Meditation is the practice of being still and focusing. It is a way to surrender, let go, and receive peace. Through meditation, by doing nothing, you can find the wisdom and strength to handle the challenges of life.

Two simple methods of meditation involve breathing and walking. They are summarized here.

> **Breathing**. Sit in a quiet place, free from distraction. Empty your hands and lap, sit up straight, and place your feet flat on the floor. (If you prefer, you may sit on the floor.) Close your eyes, lower your eyelids, or focus on one object. Count to four slowly as you breathe in. Then count to four as you breathe out. Pay attention to your breath. Empty your mind of all other thoughts. Try to keep doing this for five minutes or so. If a thought comes into your mind, just acknowledge it and let it go. Then go back to focusing on your breathing.

> **Walking**. Find a place either indoors or outside where you can walk without interruption. Walk very slowly, focusing on how your body feels as you move. Let each cycle of breathing be one step. As you breathe in, move one leg slowly forward. As you complete half of your step, let your breath out slowly until your leg lands gently on the ground. This type of meditation takes patience; there is no hurry. Empty your mind of all other thoughts. Relax your breathing. Try to disregard whatever is around you. If a thought comes into your mind or you notice something outside yourself, just acknowledge it and let it go. Then focus again on your walking. Do this for five minutes or so.

Assignment

The assignment to be completed before the next session follows:

Using any medium or format that you choose, create a representation of your new definition of masculinity. This project should express any of your ideas about what it really means to be a man. You could write a short poem, a song, or a rap. You could create a drawing or painting. You could make a collage or a clay sculpture. You may believe that you don't have any creative or artistic talent, but this assignment isn't about talent or the quality of your effort. It's about tapping into the creative part of your mind and using that aspect of yourself to expand your understanding of masculinity.

You will have the opportunity to share your project at the beginning of the next group session. However, you will not be required to share it with the group if you are uncomfortable doing so.

Reflections on Recovery

Developing a new definition of masculinity requires a process of rigorous self-examination. You need to look at your past, your present, and your desired future. You need to accept where you came from and what you've learned along the way. You need to be honest about who you are and what you really feel. You need to look at all your old behaviors and attitudes and ask which of these have worked for you and which haven't. Becoming the man that you want to be is a physical, emotional, psychological, and spiritual journey. With each step along this journey, it is important to give yourself credit for the distance that you have already traveled.

Use the space that follows to record any thoughts you have about the material covered in today's session.

Into Action

This is an optional activity. What you choose to do does not necessarily have to relate to the material covered in this session; however, it should relate in some way to your recovery.

Use the space below to describe what action step you will take between now and the next session. You also can record what results were achieved.

Creating a Vision

The "Promises of Recovery"

Creating a vision of the future does not contradict the principle of living "one day at a time." Looking forward, setting realistic goals, and investing in your future are ways to establish guidelines and direction for what you choose to do, or not do, every day. The "Big Book" of Alcoholics Anonymous addresses the future in this way:

> If we are painstaking about this phase of our development, we will be amazed before we are half way through. We are going to know a new freedom and a new happiness. We will not regret the past nor wish to shut the door on it. We will comprehend the word serenity and we will know peace. No matter how far down the scale we have gone we will see how our experience can benefit others. That feeling of uselessness and self-pity will disappear. We will lose interest in selfish things and gain interest in our fellows. Self-seeking will slip away. Our whole attitude and outlook upon life will change. Fear of people and of economic inse-curity will leave us. We will intuitively know how to handle situations which used to baffle us. We will suddenly realize that God is doing for us what we could not do for ourselves.

Are these extravagant promises? We think not. They are being ful-
filled among us sometimes quickly, sometimes slowly. They will always
materialize if we work for them.

People often call these the "promises of recovery." They do not guarantee that
your life will be free of troubles or losses or pain. They do not guarantee that you will
always get exactly what you want, when you want it. They do offer assurance that,
with the help of your higher power, you will be able to find peace, serenity, meaning,
and hope.

Gratitude

It may be difficult for you to feel a sense of gratitude at this stage of your recovery.
In your addiction, you probably were stuck in chronic feelings of anger, resentment,
envy, fear, and insecurity; focused on everything that had gone wrong and everything
that you didn't have. When you first got clean and sober, you may have been faced
with what seemed like the insurmountable task of dealing with legal and financial
consequences, repairing relationships, and putting your life back together. The truth is
that you have much to be grateful for; you just haven't had much practice in looking
at your life from a perspective of gratitude. You can develop a more positive and
grateful attitude by routinely taking the time to reflect on all the things of value in
your life.

Take some time to complete the Gratitude List that follows. Examples are

- I'm grateful that I never harmed anyone when driving drunk.
- I'm grateful that my partner is giving our relationship another chance.
- I'm grateful that I'm still alive, even if my health is poor or I'm behind bars.

The quotation is from *Alcoholics Anonymous: The Story of How Many Thousands of Men and Women Have
Recovered from Alcoholism* (4th. ed.), by Alcoholics Anonymous World Services, 2001, pp. 83–84. New York:
Alcoholics Anonymous World Services, Inc. The excerpts from Alcoholics Anonymous are reprinted
with permission of Alcoholics Anonymous World Services, Inc. ("AAWS"). Permission to reprint these
excerpts does not mean that AAWS has reviewed or approved the contents of this publication, or that
AAWS necessarily agrees with the views expressed herein. A.A. is a program of recovery from alcoholism
only—use of these excerpts in connection with programs and activities which are patterned after A.A.,
but which address other problems, or in any other non-A.A. context, does not imply otherwise.

The Gratitude List

I am grateful for these ten important things:

1.

2.

3.

4.

5.

6.

7.

8.

9.

10.

Prospective Journey

In *The Way of the Superior Man*, author David Deida writes:

> The core of your life is your purpose. Everything in your life, from your diet to your career, must be aligned with your purpose if you are to act with coherence and integrity in the world. If you know your purpose, your deepest desire, then the secret of success is to discipline your life so that you support your deepest purpose and minimize distractions and detours.
>
> But if you don't know your deepest desire, then you can't align your life to it. Everything in your life is dissociated from your core. You go to work, but since it's not connected to your deepest purpose, it is just a job, a way to earn money. You go through your daily round with your family and friends, but each moment is just another string of moments, going nowhere, not inherently profound.

In Session 4 you took a retrospective journey; you looked back at the people, events, and experiences of your life from childhood up to the time that you began this program. Now you will look forward in an activity called the Prospective Journey.

On the next page you will see the following sentence with a blank space: "It's now _____, and, as I look back over the last six months of my life, I see . . ." In that space, write what the date will be *six months from today*. If you currently are in jail or prison, you have the option of picking a date that is six months after your projected release from custody.

The page also has room for you to fill in your vision of the future. Imagine yourselves six months from now (or from your release), writing about where you are on that day and what this six-month journey has been like for you. Write in the present tense, as though you are already at that point in time. If you prefer not to write, you can draw pictures to show your journey and your life at that point.

The quotation is from *The Way of the Superior Man: A Spiritual Guide to Mastering the Challenges of Women, Work, and Sexual Desire*, by David Deida, 2004, p. 37. Boulder, CO: Sounds True. Copyright 2004 by David Deida. Reprinted with permission.

My Prospective Journey

It's now _____, and, as I look back over the last six months of my life,
I see . . .

Honoring Our Time Together

Many men are not very good at saying good-bye, especially if it involves expressing feelings of affection, respect, sorrow, or grief. You are taking the risk of letting someone know you care about him. Saying good-bye may remind you of all of the relationships you have lost or walked away from. In the *Helping Men Recover* program, you will participate in a closing ceremony. It is your opportunity to express the regard that you have for the other men and to hear them express their regard for you. In saying good-bye to each of the other men, complete the following sentences:

1. What I admire most about you is . . .
2. One thing I will remember about you is . . .
3. If I had the power to give you any gift, it would be . . .

Reflections on Recovery

Look back at the "promises" from the Big Book of Alcoholics Anonymous. These promises are for you. You have come a long way in your journey of recovery already, but your new life is just beginning. Take a few minutes to answer the questions below and to reflect on what you have experienced since you began this program. Congratulations on your effort and your work, and best wishes to you.

What are some of the things you remember doing?

What are some of the things you remember seeing?

What are some of the things you remember hearing?

What are some of the things you felt during the sessions?

What were the high points of the program for you?

What were the most difficult points?

What was the most valuable thing you gained from being in this program?

Recovery Scale

Please take a few moments to mark the degree to which you do each of the things on the scale. You assessed yourself on this scale at the beginning of this module. Please reassess yourself to see where you are now. You may want to come back to these scales as you continue in your recovery, to see the progress that you are continuing to make. Remember, recovery is a lifelong journey.

	Not at All	Just a Little	Pretty Much	Very Much
1. I acknowledge my spiritual needs.				
2. I understand the difference between religion and spirituality.				
3. I find comfort in my spiritual practices.				
4. I have a deep relationship and connection with a higher power.				
5. I feel connected to others.				
6. I respect the spiritual beliefs and practices of others.				
7. I practice some form of daily prayer or meditation.				
8. I am aware of my feelings of grief and loss.				
9. I trust my inner wisdom.				
10. I have a vision for my life.				
11. I live one day at a time.				
12. I am grateful for the life I have today.				

APPENDIX

Materials Related to Recovery

I. Five Primary Practices of the Oxford Group

The Oxford Group was a religious group that influenced the early development of Alcoholics Anonymous.

1. Confidence

Speaking truthfully

2. Confession

Saying the true and difficult things

3. Conviction

Having a sense of wrongdoing or guilt

4. Conversion

Acceptance of an altered way of life

5. Continuance

Helping others as you have been helped

II. The Twelve Steps of Alcoholics Anonymous

Alcoholics Anonymous was founded in 1935 when two alcoholics joined together to share experiences, strengths, and hopes and found that this sharing enabled them to become and remain sober. They developed the A.A. program around the following Twelve Steps of recovery:

1. We admitted we were powerless over alcohol—that our lives had become unmanageable.
2. Came to believe that a Power greater than ourselves could restore us to sanity.
3. Made a decision to turn our will and our lives over to the care of God *as we understood Him.*
4. Made a searching and fearless moral inventory of ourselves.
5. Admitted to God, to ourselves, and to another human being the exact nature of our wrongs.
6. Were entirely ready to have God remove all these defects of character.
7. Humbly asked Him to remove our shortcomings.
8. Made a list of all persons we had harmed, and became willing to make amends to them all.
9. Made direct amends to such people wherever possible, except when to do so would injure them or others.
10. Continued to take personal inventory and when we were wrong promptly admitted it.
11. Sought through prayer and meditation to improve our conscious contact with God *as we understood Him,* praying only for knowledge of His will for us and the power to carry that out.
12. Having had a spiritual awakening as the result of these steps, we tried to carry this message to alcoholics, and to practice these principles in all our affairs.

The excerpts from Alcoholics Anonymous are reprinted with permission of Alcoholics Anonymous World Services, Inc. ("AAWS"). Permission to reprint these excerpts does not mean that AAWS has reviewed or approved the contents of this publication, or that AAWS necessarily agrees with the views expressed herein. A.A. is a program of recovery from alcoholism only—use of these excerpts in connection with programs and activities which are patterned after A.A., but which address other problems, or in any other non-A.A. context, does not imply otherwise.

III. A.A. Slogans

Over the years, people in Alcoholics Anonymous have developed a number of slogans—simple phrases that people can easily remember and apply in practical ways every day. These are some of the slogans:

One Day at a Time

Let Go and Let God

Keep It Simple

Keep Coming Back

Live and Let Live

Don't Take Yourself Too Seriously

This, Too, Shall Pass

Easy Does It

IV. A Letter from Carl Jung to Bill Wilson

Bill Wilson, one of the founders of A.A., wrote to the eminent psychologist Carl Jung with a question about another man's recovery. Below is Jung's response, in which he describes the essentially spiritual nature of addiction and recovery.

Dear Mr. W.:

Your letter has been very welcome indeed.

I had no news from Roland H. anymore and often wondered what has been his fate. Our conversation, which he has adequately reported to you, had an aspect of which he did not know. The reason that I could not tell him everything was that those days I had to be exceedingly careful of what I said. I had found out that I was misunderstood in every possible way. Thus I was very careful when I talked to Roland H. But what I really thought about was the result of many experiences with men of his kind.

His craving for alcohol was the equivalent, on a low level, of the spiritual thirst of our being for wholeness, expressed in medieval language: the union with God.[1]

How could one formulate such an insight in a language that is not misunderstood in our days?

The only right and legitimate way to such an experience is that it happens to you in reality and it can only happen to you when you walk on a path which leads you to higher understanding. You might be led to that goal by an act of grace or through a personal and honest contact with friends, or through a higher education of the mind beyond the confines of mere rationalism. I see from your letter that Roland H. has chosen the second way, which was, under the circumstances, obviously the best one.

I am strongly convinced that the evil principle prevailing in this world leads the unrecognized spiritual need into perdition, if it is not counteracted either by real religious insight or by the protective wall of human community. An ordinary man, not protected by an action from above and isolated in society, cannot resist the power of evil, which is called very aptly the Devil. But the use of such words arouses so many mistakes that one can only keep aloof from them as much as possible.

These are the reasons why I could not give a full and sufficient explanation to Roland H., but I am risking it with you because I conclude from your very decent and honest letter that you have acquired a point of view above the misleading platitudes one usually hears about alcoholism.

You see, Alcohol in Latin is "spiritus," and you use the same word for the highest religious experience as well as for the most depraving poison. The helpful formula therefore is: *spiritus contra spiritum.*

Thanking you again for your kind letter

I remain yours sincerely,

C. G. Jung

[1] "As the hart panteth after the water brooks, so panteth my soul after thee, O God." (Psalm 42:1)

V. The Serenity Prayer

This prayer was first read aloud in a church service by Minister Reinhold Niebuhr in Heath, Massachusetts, in 1934. The actual author is unknown. A man who attended the church that day asked for a copy of the prayer. The minister wrote it down on a card and said that he had no further use for it. A member of A.A. found the prayer in an obituary column and showed it to Bill Wilson, the co-founder of A.A. The prayer has been used in A.A. meetings ever since.

God, grant me the serenity to accept the things I cannot change,

The courage to change the things I can,

And the wisdom to know the difference.

VI. The Synanon Prayer

Synanon was founded by Chuck and Betty Dederich in 1958. Chuck Dederich was an alcoholic and a former Gulf Oil executive who wanted a more challenging and interactive approach to sobriety than A.A. provided. He began hosting A.A. meetings with more discussion (cross-talk, or responding to someone else's story with feedback, is discouraged in A.A. meetings). For economic reasons, recovering alcoholics began living together in what came to be called a *therapeutic community*. In that community, the first heroin addicts entered recovery without medical help. Although Synanon no longer exists, therapeutic communities continue, and the model has continued to evolve as we have learned more about what works best for people with substance-use disorders.

Please let me first and always examine myself.

Let me be honest and truthful.

Let me seek and assume responsibility.

Let me understand rather than be understood.

Let me trust and have faith in myself and my fellow man.

Let me love rather than be loved.

Let me give rather than receive.

From *Basic Interface* (Vol. 1), 1994. Tucson, AZ: Amity, Inc.

VII. SMART Recovery®

SMART Recovery® is a nationwide, nonprofit organization founded by Thomas Horvath, PhD, that offers free support groups to individuals who desire to gain independence from any type of addictive behavior. SMART Recovery® also offers a free Internet Message Board discussion group and sells publications related to recovery from addictive behavior.

SMART Recovery® helps individuals gain independence from addictive behaviors (substances or activities). The 4-Point Program℠ offers specific tools and techniques for each of the following program points:

Point 1: Enhancing and Maintaining Motivation to Abstain

Point 2: Coping with Urges

Point 3: Problem Solving (managing thoughts, feelings & behaviors)

Point 4: Lifestyle Balance (balancing momentary & enduring satisfactions)

> SMART Recovery®
>
> 7537 Mentor Avenue, Suite 306
>
> Mentor, OH 44060
>
> Toll free: 866-951-5357
>
> Tel: 440-951-5357
>
> Fax: 440-951-5358
>
> E-mail: info@smartrecovery.org
>
> Web site: www.smartrecovery.org

VIII. Save Our Selves/(SOS)

Founded in 1986, SOS, also known as Secular Organization for Sobriety, addresses the needs of atheistic, agnostic, and humanistic alcoholics who like much of the program and format of A.A. but who prefer not to deal with a higher power in any form. The following are SOS's suggested guidelines for sobriety:

To break the cycle of denial and achieve sobriety, we first acknowledge that we are alcoholics or addicts.

We reaffirm this truth daily and accept without reservation the fact that, as clean and sober individuals, we cannot and do not drink or use, no matter what.

Since drinking or using is not an option for us, we take whatever steps are necessary to continue our Sobriety Priority lifelong.

A quality of life—"the good life"—can be achieved. However, life is also filled with uncertainties. Therefore, we do not drink or use regardless of feelings, circumstances, or conflicts.

We share in confidence with each other our thoughts and feelings as sober, clean individuals.

Sobriety is our Priority, and we are each responsible for our lives and our sobriety.

Save Our Selves (SOS)
4773 Hollywood Blvd.
Hollywood, CA 90027
Web site: www.sossobriety.org

ABOUT THE AUTHORS

Stephanie S. Covington, PhD, LCSW, is a nationally recognized clinician, author, and organizational consultant. With over thirty years of experience, she is noted for her pioneering work in the design and implementation of gender-responsive treatment services for women and girls in public, private, and institutional settings. She is the author of numerous books and therapeutic programs, including *A Woman's Way Through the Twelve Steps* (1994, 2009), *Beyond Trauma: A Healing Journey for Women* (2003), and *Helping Women Recover: A Program for Treating Addiction* (1999, 2008 [revised edition]), with a special edition for the criminal justice system. For the past twenty years, Dr. Covington has worked to help institutions and programs in the criminal justice system develop effective gender-responsive services. She has provided training and consulting services to the United Nations Office on Drugs and Crime, the National Institute of Corrections, the Center for Substance Abuse Treatment of the Substance Abuse and Mental Health Services Administration, the Correctional Service of Canada, the Federal Bureau of Prisons, and many state and local jurisdictions.

Dan Griffin, MA, has worked for fifteen years in Minnesota in a variety of areas in the mental health and addictions fields, including research, case management, public advocacy, teaching, and counseling. Drug courts have been the focus of his work both locally and nationally for the past eight years. The recipient of the first Hazelden fellowship, he trained as a chemical dependency counselor at Hazelden, in Center City, Minnesota, in 1999. His graduate work focused on masculinity in the Twelve Step culture. Dan is the author of *A Man's Way Through the Twelve Steps* (2009), the first gender-responsive approach to sobriety for men. Dan lives in Minneapolis, Minnesota, with his wife, Nancy, and their daughter. He has been in recovery for fifteen years.

Rick Dauer, LADC, is the clinical director at River Ridge Treatment Center in Burnsville, Minnesota. He has been a professional in the field of chemical dependence since 1984 and has experience in residential, outpatient, and corrections-based treatment programs. He has served on numerous boards, panels, and task forces dedicated to improving access to chemical dependence treatment and quality care. Rick has long been an advocate and practitioner of gender-responsive treatment, and he supervised the first pilot programs for the *Helping Women Recover* and *Helping Men Recover* curricula. Rick lives in St. Paul, Minnesota, with his wife, Julie. He has been in recovery from alcohol and drug addiction for twenty-nine years.

FEEDBACK FORM

Dear Recovering Man:

We would appreciate hearing about your experience with the *Helping Men Recover* program. Any information or feedback you would like to share with us will be greatly appreciated.

Describe yourself:

Where did you participate in this program?

Describe your overall experience with the program:

What did you find most useful?

Why? How?

What did you find least useful?

Why? How?

What was missing from the program that you wish had been covered?

Other comments or suggestions:

Thank you for your input.

Please return this survey to:
Stephanie S. Covington, PhD
Institute for Relational Development
Center for Gender and Justice
7946 Ivanhoe Avenue, Suite 201B
La Jolla, CA 92037
Fax: 858-454-8598
sc@stephaniecovington.com

Contact information for the coauthors:
Dan Griffin, MA: dan@dangriffin.com
Rick Dauer, LADC: rickdauer@aol.com

236